REBOOTING DEMOCRACY

Rebooting Democracy

A Citizen's Guide To Reinventing Politics

MANUEL ARRIAGA

Thistle Publishing

Photographs: p. 41 © Sharon Mollerus, p. 48 © Stuart Davis / Vancouver Sun, p. 50 and p. 99 © Healthy Democracy, p. 75 © Daily Express / The Mail on Sunday / The Sun / Sunday Express, p. 79 © Moderna Museet Stockholm

Cover design: Rui Silva | www.alfaiataria.org

This edition published in 2014 by Thistle Publishing.

Thistle Publishing
36 Great Smith Street
London
SW1P 3BU

ISBN: 978-1-910198-17-9

Em memória do meu pai, Filipe Arriaga.

CONTENTS

ACKNOWLEDGMENTS

In the course of this project, I was so fortunate as to benefit from the friendship, help and insights of many people. I would especially like to thank Valerie Appleby, Nikolay Archak, Erica Barbiani, Manuel Maria Carrilho, Linda Santos Costa, José Afonso Furtado, María José Gomez, Sebastien Nobert, Matthieu Ruf, Anand Swaminathan and André Trindade for their comments. Douglas J. Amy, Tom Atlee, John Dryzek and John Gastil were also so gracious as to draw on their many years of expertise and share their insights with a relative newcomer to this field. I learned much from Yoram Gat and the regular contributors to his website Equality by Lot. The invariably helpful members of the National Coalition for Dialogue and Deliberation's mailing list also pointed me in the right direction on multiple occasions. Finally, this project would not exist in its current form without the help of my agent Andrew Lownie, the assistance of David Haviland of Thistle Publishing, the illustrations of Pedro Afonso Silva and the editorial assistance of Rena Henderson.

i

REBOOTING DEMOCRACY

INTRODUCTION

> *Knowing that your vital interests are affected by factors beyond your control is a recipe for stress. It's not what democracies should be about. But it has become the new normal.* —Joris Luyendijk, author of *The Guardian*'s banking blog, reflecting on the recent financial crisis

This is a short book with a simple premise: our democracies are failing and we need to regain control of our future. I will propose five concrete measures that could allow us to do so, yet my true goal is to help initiate a public debate about how we can reform our political systems.

Who is this "we" that I write about? "We" are the citizens who find ourselves living in so-called representative democracies and increasingly questioning what that truly means. You might be Greek and trying to halt a draconian "austerity" program that is wrecking your country and that you never voted for. You might be a US citizen who opposes your administration's eagerness to embark upon yet another military adventure in the Middle East. You might be one of the millions of Brazilians who have taken to the streets, outraged with a political class that finds money to invest in sports stadiums but neglects essential public services. You might be British and still incredulous that your government has been complicit in secretly building a global surveillance machine that records everything we do online. You might be one of the many thousands of protesters who—for various other reasons—have recently come together in places as diverse as Istanbul, Kiev, Madrid, Sofia or even in the small Sussex village of Balcombe.

Or, on the contrary, you might not have particularly strong political views but still believe—like the vast majority of citizens in any "democratic" country—that the political class simply isn't accountable to the general population. The last few years have made it evident that this is no longer a concern just for a handful of activists with specific agendas. It concerns all of us.

You might call yourself a progressive, a conservative, a libertarian, an environmentalist, an anarchist or an *I-don't-believe-in-politics*-ist. It doesn't matter. Nor does it matter what angers you the most: corrupt and self-serving politicians; inaction over global warming; our nations continuously racking up debt; the erosion of your civil liberties; or the unjust wars fought in your name. What matters is that—whatever our nationality, political orientation and main grievances might be—we all realize that those who govern us do not represent us. That shared awareness unites us, and it means that we can do something about it.

♦ ♦ ♦

We live in societies gripped by palpable, widespread frustration. We all know how bogus the promise at the core of our political systems is. Yet, and without actually believing it for a second, we desperately cling to the fiction that voting every four or five years ensures that the politicians we elect will represent our interests. We try to ignore evidence to the contrary, though this realization dates back at least 250 years. Even for Rousseau, it was already evident that, in a democracy, "the . . . people believe themselves to be free, but they are gravely mistaken. They are free only during the election of their parliament. When the election is over, they become slaves again."

In today's materially affluent societies, much of our frustration stems from feeling that our lives are determined largely by external factors over which we have no control. We might oppose our government's radical measures, but against a determined political class there is little that even massive street protests can do. A majority of the population might watch in disbelief as politicians concoct an excuse to launch a military strike against some faraway nation, but no number of enraged tweets will keep the jet fighters on the ground. It may gall us to see yet another government decision favoring a business conglomerate at the expense of the public interest or another politician buying votes with expensive bridges or other public works for which future generations will pay. Yet we read it in the news, feel the bitter taste in our mouths and . . . swallow it because that is all we can do.

This sensation of powerlessness is something most of us know all too well. All over the globe, large parts of the population find themselves with no control over the crucial decisions that their political classes make, some of which will bind them for generations to come.

♦ ♦ ♦

Yet feeling we have control over our lives is a fundamental human need. In fact, a growing body of research confirms that a strong sense of autonomy is one of the essential elements for mental well-being. For psychologists working on this topic, "autonomy" has a well-defined meaning. It is not about being independent of others. Instead, autonomy means that one has substantial control over one's activities and endorses the values implicit in them. In other words, an autonomous person is a "reasonably free" agent who has a say in how things get done.

For example, studies of workplace satisfaction have found that one of the defining characteristics of a satisfying job is a sense of autonomy—that is, feeling that we have some control over how we do our job. This is something that most of us can easily relate to: when at work, few things are as frustrating and soul-deadening as having company rules and/or a supervisor who tell us exactly how we should go about the most minute aspect of our tasks, leaving us no space for choice or creativity in our work. The space for choice and "having a say" in what we do is exactly what autonomy is about and why it matters for our mental and emotional well-being.

Not surprisingly, autonomy has been found to play a key role in many other areas as diverse as how well children do in school; patient outcomes in health care; the performance of athletes; and even attempts at predicting the general levels of self-reported "happiness" across different countries. From here, it is hardly a stretch to suggest that feeling powerless over the crucial political decisions that affect us all may well be an important element of our societal malaise.

◆ ◆ ◆

If the mere *feeling* of powerlessness is causing such widespread frustration and deadening our souls, then our *actual* powerlessness is harming us in an even more direct way. Our present inability to take meaningful collective action on issues such as climate change and the fragility of the financial system threatens us in very real, palpable ways. There is widespread concern over these problems among the citizens of developed countries. Yet our political leaders seem unable—or unwilling—to deal with them in a timely manner.

If there really is such generalized frustration and un-vented anger towards our political system, one might wonder what explains the absence of widespread social un-rest. The answer to this question has two parts.

The first has to do with economics. In some regions of the world, it is still half-possible to maintain the illusion that we continue to live according to a "shared prosperity" model. This is perhaps most notably the case in some countries of northern Europe, where the combined effect of accumulated wealth, high living standards and a tradition of redistributive policies successfully masks the fact that we citizens are no longer in control.

Let's look at what has been happening in parts of the world where this mask of prosperity has slipped. A two-hour Easyjet flight is all it takes to bridge these two universes.[1] Across south-ern Europe, massive protests and social unrest have become widespread. In Athens, Madrid and Lisbon, you will hear protesters mention banks, the EU and the IMF—but, most of-ten, you will hear them accusing their *national* politicians of not truly representing the citizens who elected them.

Granted, it can be easy to read too much into rally slogans, but there seems to be a salutary and widespread awareness that it is ultimately not an economic but a *democratic* crisis that Europeans have been living through. And it is where this veil of prosperity is falling off that the true nature of our "democ-racies" becomes most visible.

The second, and probably more important, reason why this frustration hasn't yet fully materialized into a serious threat to our political system is our continued inability to propose clear, convincing alternatives. For example, we—the citizens—have to account for the paradox of the "Indigna-

---

[1] Paul Mason's *Why It's Kicking Off Everywhere: The New Global Revolutions* offers a glimpse into this other reality.

dos" and "Occupy" protest movements that successfully mobilized enormous crowds in the wake of the 2008-2010 banking crisis but seem to have (so far?) left no lasting mark on our political landscape(s). Or consider publishing phenomena such as the late Stéphane Hessel's "Indignez-vous!" in France and the anthology "Reacciona" in Spain, books that brilliantly speak to the public's frustration. Like the protest movements, these books garnered huge public attention but did not give rise to sustained social movements working towards reform.

I take the somewhat unfashionable view that much of the power of modern-day protest movements is lost whenever they fail to articulate a list of concrete demands.[2] Our repeated inability to do so has led many to believe the fiction that there are no credible alternatives, that we are stuck with the-world-as-it-is and that the best we can hope for is occasional progress in a policy domain we care about. The main goal of this book is to help foster a debate that can eventually change this state of affairs.

♦ ♦ ♦

We all have our own grievances over policy matters. Some of the more common ones have already been mentioned, but others include the decline (or, if you are lucky, stagnation) of real wages, the dismantling of social services, the way immigration is handled or any number of other important issues. My purpose here is not to engage with any of these substantive matters.

Instead, it is more important that we realize that our political system is at the root of our problems. Unfortunately, and unlike a number of worthy causes, talk of broken governance

---

[2] For the opposite argument, see David Graeber's *The Democracy Project: A History, A Crisis, A Movement*.

systems sounds positively boring. But it only seems so because we keep mistaking the forest for the trees. No matter what our personal dissatisfactions are, the ultimate problem is the fact that our politicians—for a variety of reasons discussed in the next chapter—simply do not represent us. In a sense, most social, economic and environmental ills are merely *symptoms* of this disease. Of course we should keep fighting those symptoms, but it is also about time that we start addressing the *source* from which they all stem. And that source—in all of its decidedly unsexy glory—is the profound brokenness of our democracies.

◆ ◆ ◆

Among other things, this means that voting out one politician or party to bring in a different one will *not* solve our problems. Time has made it clear that this is not merely an issue of casting. If the play stinks, replacing the actors will not make it any better.

◆ ◆ ◆

So, if our political system is the problem, what can be done about it? This book argues for five specific measures. The first four address our central concern: namely, increasing citizens' control over their government and, thus, ensuring that it acts in line with the public interest. The fifth proposal focuses on defining this very notion of "public interest" in a way that is adequately long-term oriented rather than myopic. None of these ideas has any tie to traditional notions of "left" or "right."

This book is most definitely a "version 1.0." Its goal, as mentioned earlier, is to draw attention to the problem and have us start a discussion of how to get out of this quagmire.

To be a part of that discussion and to learn about upcoming events, don't forget to join us at **http://rebootdemocracy.org**.

In the rest of the book, I will be your guide on two brief tours. The first combines insights from the social sciences with commonplace observations about our political reality. On this journey, I will introduce you to the web of interlocking mechanisms that prevents elected officials from truly representing the public interest. On the second tour, I will take you around the globe in search of ideas for reforming our democracies. We will witness the range from successful, thriving institutions to well-meaning but ultimately failed attempts at reform, not forgetting a glimpse into Soviet architecture and acrimonious nighttime meetings in an old palace in Lisbon. We will try to learn something from all of these.

Let's get started.

A Brief Detour: 10 reasons why politicians fail to represent us (and always will)

> *Why can we more easily conceive of a catastrophic event ending life on this planet than even small changes to our current economic order?* — Slavoj Žižek, in The Pervert's Guide to Ideology

Although there is widespread support for the idea that those in power do not represent the public interest, we often fail to give adequate thought to *why* this is so. Let's look at some possible explanations.

As it will become clear, I draw on varied sources. Some of the factors discussed below are recurrent themes in the media and in general political discourse; others come from well-established results in the social sciences. This diversity of perspectives is a good thing, as it promises a richer understanding of why democratic representation fails.

What nearly all of these explanations have in common, though, is that they point towards this failure having *structural* causes. In other words, the problem is in the political system itself. An improved understanding of its limitations will be helpful when considering how we can reform it.

Note: The term "public interest" will come up a lot in this book. It might be worthwhile to keep two simple insights in mind. First, and as the influential political scientist Jane Mansbridge remarked, the fact that it is famously difficult to agree on what this term means does not really reduce its practical usefulness. So, I will not be shy about using it—even if in these pages I haven't personally tried my hand at solving this ages-old philosophical debate. Second, and for reasons discussed at length in the next chapter, we can, however, confidently say that the public interest is *not* always the same as the wishes of the majority as captured, for example, in the latest opinion poll. This is an important distinction that will be useful at several points in the book.

1. Corruption

When citizens are asked why politicians fail to meet their expectations, corruption figures prominently in many of their answers. The term can, however, refer to a number of quite different phenomena, only some of which are clearly unlawful in most countries.

In its most brazen form, corruption involves the illicit exchange of money for political favors. However, the concept can also encompass conflicts of interest, as when a politician has active professional and/or financial ties to a company that he regulates. Or it could refer to substantial campaign contributions, which—even if they are legal—are likely to be "remembered" by politicians once they are in power. Finally, we can also speak of corruption when discussing the policy consequences of the pervasive "revolving door" arrangements, by which government officials know that they will likely be offered lucrative positions (e.g., as consultants or board members) in the same private-sector companies that they previously gently regulated and/or gave hefty public contracts to.

2. Electoral politics gives politicians the wrong incentives

Other problems result from politicians simply trying to be reelected. Though elections are the main mechanism through which we (periodically) control politicians, elections also provide a set of "wrong" incentives for them. A politician seeking reelection will often become a demagogue, appealing to the public's emotions, rather than their reason, to easily win their votes. Political candidates will, for the same reason, shy away from any necessary reforms that might come at an electoral cost—especially if the rationale for those reforms becomes evident only when one adopts a long-term view. Political inaction on the issue of climate change is a prime example of this.

3. Mainstream politics attracts the wrong kind of people

As of the early twenty-first century, it seems likely that most people who decide to start a professional career in politics are driven more by a pursuit of power—or, just as depressingly, a combination of ambition and a lack of comparably remunerated career alternatives—than by any genuine attachment to an ideal of public service. As a result, the political class tends to be populated by quite a peculiar group of people. This exemplifies a broader phenomenon known in the social sciences as "self-selection": when participation in an activity is voluntary, it will often end up attracting a "crowd" with particular characteristics.

If we apply this idea to those who choose a career in politics, we come up with two possibilities. The first is that, nowadays, those who join a mainstream political party and devote themselves to artfully climbing its ranks are doing so because of a strong urge to serve the public. This does not seem too likely. A second explanation seems more plausible: that self-interest and a desire for power are what drive them to enter politics. And, obviously, these are precisely the two worst possible traits for someone whose job it is to represent the public.

4. Politicians feel themselves immune to control by the public

Though it may, at first, appear to contradict the "electioneering" perils described above, the reverse also happens. In a great number of important decisions, politicians feel invulnerable to public opposition and, thus, press ahead with measures that a vast majority of the population objects to. Unfortunately for us, that often seems to be the case with major, highly contentious decisions that will affect us for several generations. In most countries, there is no mechanism for citizens to effectively block a measure being advanced by their elected government and parliament. Politicians know this and often exploit this absence of fine-grained popular control over their actions by pushing through controversial measures that the public opposes soon after taking office. Clearly, they hope that the issue will be long forgotten by the time they come up for reelection.

It is hard to overstate how perverse the combination of these two factors—electioneering perils (reason #2) and the threat of *not* being reelected failing to deter behavior against the public interest—actually is. In the worst possible way, the threat of not being reelected seems to make our politicians eager to please us in the most superficial ways (e.g., by ceding to populist demands on the scandalous topic du jour), while feeling immune to our disapproval over serious policy choices (e.g., going to war on false pretexts, signing major international treaties that severely limit national sovereignty and/or privatizing large chunks of the public sector).

5. Parties and elections morally corrupt our political leaders

Another possible explanation is that our elected leaders initially enter politics as well-meaning, public-spirited individuals but that the process through which they are selected morally corrupts them. The difficult task of rising through the ranks of their own party makes them lose sight of the common good, instead "training" them to focus on small-minded career advancement. They learn to please the higher ranks—in whose hands their future lies—at all costs. In countries in which political campaigning relies heavily on private funds, seeking campaign contributions from wealthy donors and well-funded organizations further compromises their ideals of public service. At the end of the process, actually running for office in an election also further degrades their morals. After all, winning the public's favor in a modern-day election is not easy, and the prerequisites for doing so appear to include learning how to bend the truth and taking a lax attitude towards personal or ideological loyalties.[3]

---

[3] A good illustration of the different facets of this process can be found in George Clooney's 2011 film *The Ides of March*.

6. The effect of norms on elected politicians: "politics as usual"

Besides the corrupting effect of the process through which they are selected, we also need to consider the role of what we might call the "dominant culture" in politics. Once elected, politicians do not work in a vacuum. Instead, they become a part of a professional field with its own norms, traditions and habits. As social scientists have extensively documented, someone who enters a profession will, in a variety of both conscious and unconscious ways, be subject to pressures to conform to the norms of that field. Newcomers to professional politics are no different. Even the most determined and well-meaning among them will, upon taking office, enter a world in which all social or professional interactions encourage them—subtly or not so subtly—to play along and not make too many waves. Over time, they learn to respect "the way things are usually done around here" and, ultimately, conform to the status quo.

Ironically, another part of the social norms guiding professional politics pushes people in the opposite direction—often with dire consequences. In our political culture, elected office holders feel pressure to "leave a mark" of some sort. Thus, their inclination not to rock the boat is offset by a strong desire to be known for one or two career-defining Faustian projects. These can range from major infrastructure investments to drastically reforming the nation's public sector—or even to a deadly war, always justified "for humanitarian reasons," in a faraway land. Unfortunately for us, these "projects" are undertaken in a political culture that does not support reasoned public debate. Instead, our leaders see themselves as enlightened visionaries who single-handedly bring about much-needed reform in the face of widespread opposition from "backward" citizens who "just don't understand" the need for action.

Thus, the social norms guiding professional politics succeed in simultaneously harming the public interest in two seemingly contradictory ways. Our elected politicians are both pulled towards inaction in matters where change is required and encouraged to make "daring" major decisions without public consultation. Unfortunately, experience strongly suggests that such bouts of proactivity by elected leaders in the face of public disapproval only very rarely work to our benefit. Much more often, they appear to serve either the private interests of the politicians' associates or merely their need for self-aggrandizement.

7. The psychological effects of power and identification with other elites

The social sciences offer us two other insights into how politicians operate. These have to do with power and what happens when politicians spend time dealing with other influential individuals.

First, social psychologists have found that individuals who experience a sense of power become less able to empathize with others. Politicians, by virtue of their jobs, are likely to perceive themselves as power holders and, thus, to be unable to adopt the perspective of those affected by their decisions. As their political careers develop over the years, and they come closer to attaining positions of greater power, politicians will gradually become less and less able to put themselves in the shoes of the average citizen.

Second, we know that a sense of identification with a social group—i.e., perceiving oneself as "belonging" to a certain group—is a powerful determinant of attitudes and behavior. Individuals identify with groups with whom they believe they share significant traits. The result can range anywhere from calling yourself British to emphasizing your ethnic background or even simply saying you are a supporter of your local football club. Those would all be examples of more "explicit" forms of self-categorization. However, sometimes identities can also take more "latent" or "implicit" forms. Think, for example, of an immigrant developing a new sense of national identity or someone who recently switched careers. In those (and other) situations, individuals can combine within themselves several identities, sometimes without even being fully aware of it. Needless to say, we all categorize ourselves—be it in more or less conscious fashion—into a variety of groups.

What happens next, though, is even more interesting. A body of work in social psychology known as "social identity theory" describes how, once people identify with a certain group, that sense of belonging significantly affects their attitudes and behavior. They develop an increasingly positive image of fellow group members. They experience a sense of loyalty to the group and exhibit, either consciously or unconsciously, a much greater inclination to help and cooperate with other group members. At the same time, group members start to perceive members of the "out-group"—i.e., those who are seen as *not* belonging to the group—in a less positive way and find it increasingly difficult to empathize with them. As a result, the group member becomes less prone to help and cooperate with them.

These ideas can help us understand the behavior of our elected political class. We know that, over the course of their duties, acting politicians will spend many of their waking hours dealing with members of other powerful elites. They will, for example, spend vast amounts of time interacting with representatives of large corporations and other established interest groups.

We can easily envision how this process unfolds. Locked in meeting rooms with members of the business sector for countless hours, our elected representatives will, over time, develop a shared sense of belonging to something we might call the "economic-political elite." After all, the actions of politicians and business leaders jointly determine many of the crucial decisions we collectively care about. It is only natural that, over the course of time, most politicians will start to see business leaders as their peers in the process of policy-making.

Employing the lessons of social identity theory, it becomes easy to predict what happens next. Politicians become increasingly sympathetic to the arguments presented by the other members of this elite they belong to. Over time, they adopt, more and more, the logic of business, and the demands/arguments of other groups will become harder and harder to understand. Perhaps most distressing is that this process can take place in a largely unconscious way. Politicians themselves might often be unaware of the ties and the growing sense of identification that they are developing with their peers in the business community; yet, whether or not they are aware, the consequences will be just as real.

Therefore, we have at least two distinct psychological mechanisms that can help us understand how our elected politicians will, over time, become increasingly unable to adopt the perspective of the common citizen—and all the while their way of thinking will continue to grow closer and closer to that of other powerful factions in society.

8. Ideology as a bias

However, it is not just a sense of power and identification with other elites that can bias politicians' reasoning. Powerful ideas warp the way we think, too—especially when those ideas are fundamental to our way of seeing the world or we are known for espousing them.[4]

As cognitive psychologists have learned, we are very good at filtering information according to how well it fits our worldview. In a process known as "confirmation bias," we tend to welcome all information that validates our preconceptions and to discredit any that challenges our thinking. This process largely ensures that we will tend to (re)*confirm* our views and continue acting according to them—even when evidence overwhelmingly points in a different direction.

A discussion of "ideology" will seem strange to some, given that many tend to think that modern-day politicians are mostly free of sincere political convictions and are mainly engaged in a mixture of optimizing their chances of reelection and catering to private interests. This view is correct, but even spineless politicians operate within a set of beliefs about how the world works—beliefs that they might have picked up from their colleagues, party elders or simply the broader political milieu. It is in that sense that we can speak of them being "ideological."

This—and the dramatic effect it can have on public policy—is so painfully clear as of 2014. In recent years, both sides of the Atlantic have lived through an ill-timed drive for "austerity" or "deficit cutting" that has threatened to

---

[4] Admittedly, we all tend to reserve the word "ideology" for those ideas we disagree with. In this section, I will use it to refer to ideas that seem to fly in the face of most available evidence and, yet, are so strong that they seem largely unaffected by it.

cripple the economy and (at least in the case of Europe) keep many millions of young people in long-term unemployment. The amazing thing is that the "political consensus" that has emerged among mainstream politicians has flown in the face of nearly everything we know about economics, as well as the public views of countless respected economists.

For example, regarding the US fiscal debate, Nobel-prize-winning economist Paul Krugman wrote that it was "dominated by *things everyone knows* that happen not to be true." One of them is the notion that the US was going through a fiscal crisis *in the first place*. Similarly, Joseph Stiglitz, yet another Nobel laureate in economics, remarked that in Europe, "the cure is not working and there is no hope that it will," calling austerity measures "deeply misguided."

Obviously, several other factors influenced the behavior of the European and US political classes. However, much of what we witnessed was the result of ideology—often with the undertones of a morality play—winning out over reason and evidence.

A narrative built on feelings of guilt and a need to atone for alleged past sins—years of "living above our means"; a public that was complicit in the "irresponsible," "spend-thrift" ways of earlier governments; etc.—was a common theme across the Atlantic. In the US, it got combined with a general ideological discomfort among its political class with the idea of public spending. In Europe, it blends in with the sacralization of the Euro, made clear in the words of Mario Draghi, the president of the European Central Bank, when he said that the European leadership would do "whatever it takes" to ensure the survival of the common currency. Other ideological elements are the deep-seated, extreme aversion of German politicians (and, by implication, the ECB) to any risk of inflation and, on the part of a subset of European politicians, the desire to use this crisis as an opportunity for dismantling parts of the state.

In both cases, the insularity of our political classes—and the way they exert power from the comfort of the little "bubble" in which they live—leaves them and their preconceptions safely unchallenged. Thus, inherited notions continue to shape the debate and guide public policy over crucial matters, without pesky reality getting in the way.

9. The political class is not demographically representative of the general population

These issues are further complicated by the simple fact that the political class is, in demographic terms, highly unrepresentative of the general citizenry. It will come as no surprise that, in most of our countries, the average politician is a white male with a comparatively privileged socio-economic background.

In and of itself, this is not necessarily a problem: it is conceivable that—*with adequate checks and controls*—a politician meeting that description could truly represent the interests of the general population. However, given the lack of strong accountability mechanisms, serious problems arise from the fact that the vast majority of our political representatives effectively belong to a separate caste. Members of this caste are extremely unlikely to ever suffer from many of the issues that plague significant parts of the population (e.g., difficulty paying the bills, the threat of unemployment, lack of adequate health care or worries about street crime in their neighborhood). They know perfectly well that holding an elected post will ensure their livelihoods well into the future, in the form of cozy public- sector and/or corporate appointments once they no longer succeed in getting reelected.

As one might expect, this huge gap between the life conditions of our rulers and the reality inhabited by large parts of the population means that it is very difficult for politicians to even grasp the consequences of many of their decisions on the lives of citizens. And if merely *grasping* those consequences is already that hard, then it is virtually hopeless that politicians would be able to experience the empathy required to fully gauge the consequences of their decisions.

Not surprisingly, in demographic terms, our political class is remarkably similar to another relevant group: the same business elite—and the representatives of other powerful established interests—we discussed earlier. Those meeting rooms where they all get together are largely populated by white males used to a privileged life. In several countries, most of them will even be alumni of the same two or three prestigious universities.

As described earlier, the psychological process of identification with a group—and its pernicious consequences—is fueled by the sharing of traits between the individual and other group members. The large extent to which our elected representatives and those speaking on behalf of big business share demographic traits and/or backgrounds is yet another reason to fear that our representatives will unduly identify with members of that other group and, thus, fail to adequately represent us.

10. Perhaps the world functions in such a way that politicians' hands are effectively tied

An altogether different explanation also needs to be included in this list. It is possible that what we perceive as the gap between what our elected leaders do and the public interest is not actually due to some perversion of their mandates but, instead, to the sheer impossibility of acting in a fundamentally different way. Perhaps politicians, once they take office, discover that they are largely impotent to change even relatively minor aspects of how our societies function. This powerlessness could be due to various factors.

It could stem from the need to negotiate with other political actors (e.g., by striking a deal with other parties in order to secure approval in parliament for a given measure). This need for political compromise between parties helps explain why our representatives might not succeed in bringing about real change.

Or it could be due to the political dependence of our elected leaders on the business sector. As political scientists have been discussing for the past forty years, in our societies, the government is largely dependent on the private sector when it comes to job and wealth creation. These also happen to be the two main criteria by which the general population judges the government when election time arrives. (As Bill Clinton's campaign strategist famously put it, "[it's] the economy, stupid.") Combined, these two elements ensure that our elected leaders will necessarily be quite eager to cater to the interests of the business sector; otherwise, business will suffer, unemployment will rise and the politicians' chances of reelection will be severely hampered.

A modern variant of this same argument stresses the interconnectedness of our economies. According to its proponents, if a government adopts measures that the business sector deems less than desirable, then corporations will simply shift their activity to some other place on the globe, leaving in their wake unemployment and a missed opportunity for increasing local prosperity. At the same time, global financial markets might "punish" the offending country by demanding higher interest rates for loans to people and businesses based there, which would, in turn, wreak further havoc on its economy.

Finally, yet another way in which our leaders might be powerless is by virtue of international agreements and/or membership in international institutions. According to this argument, belonging to bodies such as the European Union and World Trade Organization puts severe limits on what political leaders might achieve. An increasing number of decisions are made at the supranational level, and national governments have little choice but to implement them.

◆ ◆ ◆

As I already pointed out, these factors interact with each other in a variety of ways. One example is how electoral considerations contribute to several of the other problems identified above. Obviously, maximizing their chances of reelection plays a key role in cultivating a short-term, demagogical orientation among our leaders. It also makes them particularly eager to play the internal power games within their party to the best of their advantage—no matter how much they might need to compromise their principles in the process. Electoral considerations can also go as far as making many political measures (seem) utterly impossible to put into practice. For example, the prospect of negative media coverage discussing job losses caused by a new piece of environmental regulation can make its adoption politically unviable—and thus contribute to the "politicians' hands are tied" syndrome.

Similarly, a variety of these factors combine to explain the often-suspect proximity of our political leaders to the corporate world. One part of the story is their dependence on the business sector to generate levels of economic growth that will smooth the way to reelection. Another has to do with demographic and psychological factors, such as the similarity and strong sense of identification between members of our political and economic elites. Finally, any instance of corruption—no matter whether it is more- or less-overt—will also further cement that relationship, as will a political culture that tolerates it.

When we look at the big picture—i.e., these different factors interacting with one another—it is hard to imagine a mischievous deity coming up with a political system that could possibly be *worse*-equipped than our current one to address the serious challenges facing us. What we *can* be confident of is that only under rare conditions would a professional politician ever take any action that would risk affecting her country's position in the reigning international political/economic order. One consequence of this is that pressing global issues—such as regulating an out-of-control financial sector and addressing climate change, to name but two examples—have little chance of making substantial progress outside of the murky, unreliable processes of international conferences.[5]

♦ ♦ ♦

With this said, things get interesting—and worrisome—when some of the major behavioral drivers governing the political class pull in opposite directions. This is the situation

---

[5] As David Runciman argues in *The Confidence Trap: A History of Democracy in Crisis from World War I to the Present,* our democracies *do* have a track record of eventually addressing crucial issues—but only when these problems have escalated into full-blown crises and push society to a breaking point. Obviously, this provides little comfort. How long until our leaders badly miscalculate the need for urgent action? And—for those who take this as evidence of how "self-correcting" and "adaptable" our democracies are—who will be held accountable for all the avoidable human suffering incurred while politicians drag their feet?

in which Europeans have recently found themselves, and it provides an exemplary case study of the limitations of electoral politics.[6]

The European financial crisis has placed the continent's political class in the crossfire between what are perhaps the two central drivers of its behavior: conformity to the international economic order and the desire not to openly antagonize large numbers of voters to a level that will generate electoral backlash (or even more serious social unrest). Both are ultimately forms of fear, as we will see.

All politicians (in northern and southern Europe alike) fear the consequences of challenging the ruling economic order. In short: the Euro must be preserved at all costs; the European Central Bank's mandate will remain largely unchanged; and sovereign debts are to be honored.

In northern European countries, electoral considerations cause politicians to also fear being seen as enabling "handouts" or displaying "forgiveness" towards the "lazy," indebted southerners. This means that northern politicians will be very reluctant to take the steps that could restore the viability of the ruling economic order. At the same time, many of their private banks (and their broader economies) will be in deep trouble if southern nations collapse and abandon the Euro in a "disorderly" way. They are, thus, in a bind.

In southern European countries, something equally (if not *more*) perverse is happening. Politicians fear the electoral repercussions of imposing the cuts demanded by their northern sponsors. But most of them fear *even more* the electoral consequences of being held responsible for their countries leaving the Euro zone.

---

[6] Readers to whom the recent European crisis is of no special interest can skip over these final paragraphs without hesitation. They are included merely as an illustration of the ideas discussed earlier in this chapter.

In the face of such a serious threat to the prosperity of the whole continent, the European political class is paralyzed by fear. For now, they seem unable to take either of the two viable courses of action: 1) salvaging the economies of the indebted nations appears impossible because substantial debt haircuts are off the table, inflation remains a taboo and the leaders in northern countries are unable to commit to the mutualization of sovereign debt and assume shared responsibility for future bank rescues; and 2) having southern countries abandon the Euro and go back to their former national currencies in an orderly manner seems impossible because no office-holding southern European politician dares to consider it as an option.

In the middle of all this noise, the bigger questions naturally are forgotten. In particular, it is easy to forget the extent to which this entire situation is the result of another epic failure of democratic representation. The European political elite introduced the Euro in 1999 through a project that largely sidelined the European citizenry. At the time, our Promethean leaders were so collectively enamored of the "Great European Project" that they pressed ahead, paying little attention to the serious concerns of countless economists and the skepticism of much of the population. Almost twenty years later, in the midst of yet another wave of highly undemocratic decision-making, Europeans are now asked to collectively pay the price for these follies.[7]

---

[7] Recent events in countries such as Poland and Latvia attest just how powerful these forces really are. With the extreme gravity of the European financial crisis plain for all to see, political leaders in both of these nations are aggressively pushing for their countries to adopt the Euro, even in face of widespread public opposition.

DELEGATION AND IRREFLECTION: THE TWIN ROOTS OF FAILED POLITICAL REPRESENTATION

Having sketched out the ways in which political representation is bound to continue failing us, let me pause briefly to ask what lies at the source of these problems. After all, and as most of us learned in school, representative democracy promised to be an effective solution to the challenge of public governance.

At the heart of this book lies the notion that there are twin causes for these problems.

Delegation

The first of these is our unquestioning faith in delegation. Being able to delegate tasks to others is obviously a vital aspect of our societies. However, delegation can work only if there are mechanisms in place to ensure the proper alignment between the wishes of the person delegating the task (in economics jargon, the "principal") and the actions of her representative (the "agent").

These mechanisms can take a variety of forms. One would be incentives to perform well: if the agent's performance can be easily and reliably evaluated, then the principal can set goals for the agent to achieve and agree to reward (or punish) him accordingly.

Another driver of the agent's "good behavior" can be social norms. Even in the absence of oversight, social norms—such as a culture that promotes honesty, professionalism or, in the specific case of politics, a commitment to an ideal of public service—will often induce the agent to act according to the principal's best interests.

A third important factor in aligning the interests of the principal and the behavior of the agent can be emotional ties. The existence of a mutually treasured relationship between the two parties—or even just a sense of identification between the agent and the principal—will often succeed in making delegation work.

With regard to the issue of political representation, how well can these three mechanisms work for us? Might they actually be effective in making politicians truly represent the public interest? The answer, unfortunately, is not very encouraging. Let's see why they are likely to fail us.

Emotional ties, or even just a mere sense of identification, between members of our political class and the general population won't help us much. As argued in the previous chapter, most politicians belong to a caste that lives in a world quite different from that of the bulk of the population. They will have few reasons to care for—or identify with—those on the other side of that divide. In fact, they are most likely to identify with *other elites* in our society, not with the general citizenry. This means that emotional ties will, if anything, *worsen* the chances of delegation working as we intended it to.

Nor can we rely on social norms. Even if, in some parts of the globe, there arguably existed, at some point in the second half of the twentieth century, a true culture of public service, evidence suggests that it is now almost universally extinct. If media accounts are any indication, a culture of cutthroat electioneering and PR strategizing currently dominates the field of professional politics. It is, thus, highly unlikely that social norms of (for example) "serving the public interest" will ensure proper behavior by the political class.

This brings us to the central issue of how well incentives (coupled with an oversight mechanism) can help us keep tabs on the political class. After all, that's precisely what our representative democracies place their faith in.

In the case of political representation, a politician's prime incentive for good behavior is being reelected. Elections are the oversight mechanism: according to one of the central myths of our democracies, that is the time when citizens "pass judgment" on the performance of the incumbent leaders/party and collectively decide whether they are worthy of reelection.

Now, to evaluate how reasonable our collective faith in this mechanism really is, briefly entertain the following analogy. We will take our cue from introductory courses in microeconomics, in which the principal-agent problem is commonly presented by adopting the perspective of a shop owner (the principal) who decides to hire a manager (the agent) to supervise the daily operation of his business.

The question we should ask ourselves is: in the absence of strong social norms and/or an emotional tie between the two, how reasonable is it to expect that the manager will perform his job satisfactorily if the shop owner were to drop by the store every four years to check on how well business is going? Would anyone be amazed if, under these conditions, the manager were to disregard the interests of the shop owner, only quickly trying to cover up his lack-adaisical or self-enriching behavior right before the shop owner's visit?

Even though this situation already looks bad enough—you might ask yourself if you would ever consider becoming a partner in such a store—the reality of political representation is far worse. To get a grasp of why that is so, let's continue with the shop analogy. Doing so will introduce us to the second cause of failed political representation.[8]

Decision-making without reflection

We already know that the owner thinks it is enough to drop by every four years. Now, suppose that, when he does so, he merely takes a cursory glance at the manager's performance and takes neither the time nor the effort to reflect on the manager's decisions and how they have impacted his business. The owner neglects to study the accounting books or to hear what others can tell him about how well the business is being run. Instead, he lets his "instincts" (or "gut feelings") determine his evaluation of the manager's performance.

In a similarly thoughtless manner, during his brief visits to the store, the owner also considers the option of having the manager replaced. In line with his general approach, he

---

[8] Before proceeding, though, it is worthwhile to highlight that misplaced expectations regarding delegation are a much broader problem that is also starkly present in the corporate world. In recent years, there has been talk of a "shareholder spring" (shareholders rising in protest against excessive executive compensation), but the depth of the problem is perhaps even better illustrated by the continued reckless behavior at banks. Whenever managers and the traders they oversee sustainedly engage in practices that put the very existence of the whole bank at stake—thus risking wiping out all the capital invested by shareholders whose interests they supposedly represent—our notions of delegation deserve some serious rethinking. These problems are addressed at length in *The Battle for the Soul of Capitalism* by John Bogle (founder of Vanguard, one of the world's largest mutual fund companies) and his later joint work with Alfred Rappaport (professor at the Kellogg Graduate School of Management at Northwestern University), *Saving Capitalism From Short-Termism*.

quickly reaches a decision on this issue, too: he skims the resumés of a couple of job candidates and soon makes up his mind whether any of them intuitively strikes him as "serious" and "up to the job."

♦ ♦ ♦

It's quite obvious what is wrong with the shop owner's behavior. His coming bankruptcy will be due to a combination of two factors: first, he delegated control of his store to the manager and, second, he believed that a cursory, unreflective and "gut-driven" overview of the manager's performance every four years would be enough to keep the business on course.

The parallel with our system of political representation should be obvious. When we are asked, in an election, to "evaluate" how well our politicians have been serving us, we do a similarly poor job. We all, including "informed" citizens who follow the news, neglect to thoroughly study the most important policy issues. We vote for a candidate based largely on what are little more than "gut feelings" regarding her honesty and reasonableness. At best, we have picked up a few tidbits from friends and the media that we take as truly revealing of that candidate's character.

These already precarious judgments are also considerably influenced by how much sympathy each of us has for the party a given politician represents. Here, again, the powerful psychological mechanism of identification rears its head (we met it before in our discussion of how politicians will tend to identify with other elites). In this case, social identification almost inevitably leads us to exaggerate the virtues of politicians belonging to the party we favor. Conversely, we tend to find the faults of the other parties' representatives particularly damning. Again, we often reach these conclusions unconsciously, and these processes influence our judgments without us even being aware of them. As one might expect, our ability to competently judge the performance of politicians at election time is, thus, further weakened.

It should be clear that we voters are not to "blame" for our failure to adequately judge the performance of our representatives. After all, doing so would require us to engage in a careful analysis of the policy issues facing our societies. Only then could we properly evaluate our politicians according to how well they performed on those issues. But the truth is that it is simply not realistic to expect citizens to engage in that kind of in-depth analysis.

Look at this from the perspective of any individual citizen. The amount of information that she would need to analyze to reach an adequately informed decision about just a handful of major policy issues is staggering. In a representative democracy, that same citizen knows that her single vote is bound to have only the tiniest impact on the outcome of an election—after all, she is just one among millions of voters. The amount of work involved in thoroughly analyzing a policy issue/option, combined with the extremely low likelihood that a single vote will significantly affect the outcome of an election, makes it reasonable for individual voters to abstain from digging deep into any issues. That is why political scientists speak of voters' "rational ignorance": in a modern-day representative democracy, it simply does not pay for the voter to be fully informed on policy issues.

♦ ♦ ♦

Even if we somehow managed to overcome rational ignorance, and citizens developed an inclination to be "reasonably good shop owners" who gather some of the available information before making election decisions, matters wouldn't necessarily be significantly better.

Virtually all voters will still rely on their own *individual* consumption of information *from secondary sources* when forming an opinion about a politician or policy topic. Media reports, arguments by interest groups in favor/against a given politician or policy measure, and the public statements of politicians, commentators and other opinion-makers are all likely to play a key role in shaping voters' views. This introduces a number of interrelated problems that are very difficult to overcome.

The cornerstone of these problems is that this wealth of information will tend to be processed by individuals in largely the same "snap," unreflective manner that currently plagues most voters' judgment of politicians. We read a couple of articles, perhaps catch a debate on TV and form "an opinion."

While doing so, we favor some media outlets or commentators over others, deeming some as trustworthy and others as less reliable. Likewise, we label specific news stories as important and credible, while relegating others to the back of our minds. We do all this in a largely unconscious way.

Remember our earlier discussion of "confirmation bias"? We will accept and believe news and other information that agrees with our worldview, while we will tend to discount any conflicting evidence. This largely ensures that, even if voters tried to be better-informed on matters, they would quite likely end up merely reinforcing their pre-existing, "intuitive" views on the issue(s).

To get a notion of how precarious the "opinions" we all form really are, consider that virtually none of them will ever be subject to the rigors of even the most basic adversarial challenge.[9]

---

[9] At least beyond the casual exchange of a couple of provocative

Most of us would agree that, when facing an important decision, it is quite reasonable to ask others for feedback and, hopefully, have a reasoned discussion about which course to take. With the benefit of their insights and experiences, you stand a very real chance of improving the quality of your decisions.

However, voters' political views rarely, if ever, get exposed to the light of day. In fact, they have quite a dark, depressing life cycle: they emerge from a murky, deeply flawed information-gathering process, live a largely unquestioned existence in the depths of their carrier's mind and, finally, seep out to leave their mark on a secret ballot. With the exception, perhaps, of mushrooms, nothing good grows in the dark. So, it should be evident that opinions formed this way are at odds with the kind of careful, reasoned decision-making required of citizens when it comes to politics.[10]

♦ ♦ ♦

A second, closely related problem with the way we voters decide on political matters is that, by basing our views on our private "digestion" of information coming from secondary sources, we collectively become easy prey for manipulation by special-interest groups. The reason for this

---

remarks between friends or family members of different political persuasions, both of whom are guaranteed to stick to well-defined roles during the exchange—e.g., "the liberal" and "the conservative"—and none of them actually considering the content of the other's remarks.

[10] In recent years, the virtues of spontaneous, instinctive decision-making have been popularized in books such as Malcolm Gladwell's *Blink: The Power Of Thinking Without Thinking*. I hope it is easy to (intuitively!) recognize that complex policy issues (e.g., how to properly regulate the financial sector) don't quite have an "intuitively evident" solution.

is that any "encounter" between a voter and these secondary sources will necessarily be a highly asymmetric one.

Discussing markets as distinct as the global cotton trade and modern-day financial markets, the economic sociologist Michel Callon has described how an "uneven distribution of calculative capabilities" commonly leads to market power and transactions that most would deem as "rigged." In the age of high-frequency trading, for example, no amateur day-trader—no matter how skilled—is a match for hedge funds armed with dozens of brilliant mathematicians and powerful computers. It is important that we come to realize that the "electoral market"—i.e., the market for votes in which our futures are decided—is equally rigged. Given the resources available to the political class and special-interest groups, the political views of each of us (taken in isolation) are easy prey.

Politicians and special-interest groups invest large amounts of time, effort and other resources into making their public image as appealing as possible to large segments of the population. They hire PR professionals and run countless focus groups to test variations of their "message," subsequently honing it according to the feedback they receive from these groups so that the average voter will take its main points as "intuitively true" and, thus, will leave them unquestioned. And they spend enormous amounts of money to guarantee that this message is delivered to you in the format—and at the time and place—that is most likely to have an impact on your voting behavior.

Think about the average voter, who is busy going about her life—juggling work and family issues while trying to complete all the tasks on her to-do list. Time for reflection and pondering is not something she has a lot of. Now, add to this picture a flurry of expertly crafted political messages, each of them promoting a different candidate and all targeted at her. To think that the outcome of this process might be even remotely described as a reasoned, careful pondering of different political points of view is very optimistic, to say the least. Yet, incredibly, we stick to the fiction that elections provide us with an adequate mechanism to accurately evaluate and compare the political options presented to us.

Perhaps the closest analogue is that of entering a modern-day supermarket believing that you will buy "strictly what you need." While walking down an aisle, you are bombarded with a variety of stimuli carefully engineered to induce largely unconscious responses that will lead to impulse shopping. Even the physical layout of the store itself is the result of many hours spent studying how to maximize the number of products you are exposed to and the amount of time you will spend inside it—since the more products you walk past and the longer your visit, the more you are likely to buy.

As voters, we are likewise stuck on the receiving end of this kind of deeply asymmetric "cognitive warfare." An intelligent, well-meaning voter who relies on the passive, individual consumption of secondary sources is condemned to be largely overpowered by the combination of vast resources and state-of-the-art marketing techniques aimed at influencing his views. Competition among different political messages will, at best, result in the party with the most appealing message—often the one with the largest marketing budget—winning the public vote. And we can easily agree that is not what a democracy should be run on.

As long as our political systems relegate us to the role of a voter who relies on "gut feelings" and secondary sources of information, we will be vulnerable to rhetoric and manipulation. Thus, we will continue to be unable to critically engage with the messages we are exposed to, and politicians and special-interest groups will continue to have their way.

♦ ♦ ♦

In summary, there are two problems at the root of the failure of democratic representation:

1) We have *delegated power* to the political class and hardly supervise it.

2) As voters, we are condemned to *unreflective and easy-to-influence decision-making*. Even if we were inclined to effectively supervise politicians, this would severely limit our ability to do so.

Together, these problems present a real challenge. On the one hand, we can entrust power to a political elite who is able to minimally ponder policy issues—but who is also almost totally unaccountable to the general population. (This is what we have been doing so far.) On the other, we can give voters a stronger voice through, for example, a more direct form of democracy, but the risk is that they will speak in an uninformed, non-thinking way. Neither seems an especially promising approach.

♦ ♦ ♦

Let's return for a moment to the hypothetical case of a shop owner and his manager. Some of you may have felt—rightly so—that the comparison was an oversimplification. After all, the shop belongs to a single individual, while, in our societies, millions of us are ultimately in charge.

At first sight, this adds a whole other layer of complexity to the problem: it introduces a need for collective decision-making. If the shop were, in fact, owned by millions of people, then the issue would no longer simply be how to ensure that the manager's actions are in line with the owners' interests. Before worrying about that, the owners would first need to collectively agree on *what they want*. More concretely, they would need to find a way to jointly decide on matters and speak with a single voice.

At the core of this book lies the notion that this additional difficulty actually holds the key to solving the *other* problems we've already identified (that is, ensuring effective representation and avoiding thoughtless decision-making). That key is *citizen deliberation*, and we will come back to it repeatedly throughout the rest of this book.

#1 DISCOVERING CITIZEN DELIBERATION IN THE PACIFIC NORTHWEST

> *Politics is the rare sport where the amateur is better than the professional.* —Lawrence Lessig, professor at Harvard Law School, interviewed in 2011

Suppose that you lived in a world thirsting for cheap and non-polluting energy sources. Imagine, further, that we had, at several points in history, *known* how to produce energy in a way that was simultaneously safe, clean and affordable.

Unfortunately for us, this knowledge was mostly forgotten over the centuries and, thus, this technology had disappeared from mainstream use. We found ourselves forced to rely on dirtier and more dangerous ways to obtain energy.

In some remote parts of the world, though, this technology had been revived and was currently being used successfully. There was also a vibrant community of academics and practitioners who, for several decades, had been working out the details of how to best use this technology and the ways in which it could be further improved.

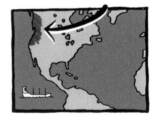

What I will argue in this chapter (and, more broadly, throughout this book) is that the little-known practice of citizen deliberation similarly has the potential to help us address one of the fundamental challenges facing us today. It might not be quite on the scale of cold fusion—but, luckily for us, it is not quackery, either.

◆ ◆ ◆

So what is citizen deliberation and how can we make use of it? The fundamental idea is a radically simple one. A group of ordinary citizens is tasked with collectively deciding on a policy matter. They consult with experts, listen to advocates representing different interest groups and, with the assistance of skilled facilitators, engage in careful, reasoned group discussions in which they explore the issues at hand. Throughout the entire process, the citizen panel is autonomous and its actions self-directed: it decides on, for example, the information it needs to gather from external sources, which experts or advocates to interview and what questions to ask them. A professional administrative and research staff assists the citizens in these duties.

After an adequate deliberation period, the group makes a collective decision on the topic by taking a vote and then issues a public statement. Its decision can be integrated into our existing political structures in several different ways, some of which we will review at the end of this chapter.[11]

Now, how does one go about selecting ordinary citizens to participate in these deliberative panels? *One doesn't.* Citizens are recruited from the electorate *at random*—the same way they get called up for jury duty in Anglo-Saxon (and other) countries—and then are appointed for a single, non-renewable term.

---

[11] It should be clear from the outset, though, that these citizen panels should have more power than merely producing "recommendations" for the benefit of the government and/or the state bureaucracy.

The kleroterion was used in ancient Athens to randomly select citizens for political duty.

This may seem crazy at first. For many, it conjures up images of raucous popular assemblies where spirits run wild, and only those who shout the loudest get heard. Readers who followed the debate about healthcare reform in the US might remember such sorry scenes from the "town hall meetings" held in the summer of 2009, many of which quickly degenerated into little more than shouting matches. Rest assured that what I propose in this chapter bears no relation to that.

Although most of us have never heard of citizen deliberation, the use of a lottery to select citizens for political duty dates back to ancient Athens, where it was an established practice. The Greeks understood that choosing individuals from the citizenry at random is the only way to defend against the different forms of corruption that plague a professional political class. By entrusting power to a panel of

41

citizens drawn by lot and having them serve a single, non-renewable term, most of the problems described in the second chapter of this book can be avoided. Free from the pressure of seeking reelection, on the one hand, and from the biases inherent in being part of a powerful elite, on the other, randomly chosen citizens are able to pursue what best serves the public interest.[12]

♦ ♦ ♦

With an understanding of the rationale for randomly recruiting citizens, the question that immediately comes to mind is whether ordinary citizens have what it takes. Can they possibly be smart enough? To the surprise of many, this turns out to be an unfounded concern. Over the last three decades, countless citizen panels have been convened all over the world, and experience tells us that, if the process is set up in the right way, citizen panels are perfectly capable of analyzing and deciding on complex policy matters.

Skeptical? Let us survey what some leading scholars in the field of citizen deliberation have written on the topic:

---

[12] In the wake of the Occupy movement, some argued that "popular assemblies," in which all citizens who wished to do so would be able to freely participate in the decision-making process, could also help us avoid those problems. However, they are plagued by their own serious difficulties. First, popular assemblies do not scale to a large society. Second, they are vulnerable to manipulation by powerful interests who are able to more effectively organize and sponsor the participation of their own supporters. Third, when all are invited to talk, often only the most motivated—and most extreme—voices will make the effort to be heard. Although it might seem paradoxical at first, a random few are preferable to the unfiltered many when it comes to representing the totality of the public.

- In a comprehensive survey of empirical studies on citizen deliberation, John Dryzek (professor of political science at the Australian National University) observes that the "first lesson" to be drawn from these studies is that of "citizen competence." In his words: "[T]he most obvious finding is that, given the opportunity, ordinary citizens can make good deliberators. Moreover, issue complexity is no barrier to the development and exercise of that competence."

- After two decades of running citizen panels, James Fishkin (professor of political science and communication at Stanford) believes that "the public is very smart if you give it a chance. If people think their voice actually matters, they'll do the hard work, really study . . ., ask the experts smart questions and then make tough decisions. When they hear the experts disagreeing, they're forced to think for themselves. About 70% change their minds in the process." "[C]itizens can become better informed and master the most complex issues of state government if they are given the chance."

- After their 2010 in-depth study of two citizen panels, John Gastil (professor of communication at Penn State University) and doctoral researcher Katherine Knobloch concluded that participants engaged in "high-quality deliberation" characterized by a "rigorous analysis of the issues." These citizens "carefully analyzed the issues put before them and maintained a fair and respectful discussion throughout the proceedings." The statements produced by the two citizen panels at the end of the process "included almost all of the key insights and arguments that emerged during their meetings, and . . . were free of any gross factual errors or logical fallacies."

Drawing on his many years of research on citizen deliberation, Gastil didn't find this surprising at all: in his words, such displays of political competence by ordinary citizens are simply the "typical result for a very well-structured deliberative event."

◆ ◆ ◆

Remember that, in these panels, citizens are not left to discuss and decide on policy matters based just on their prior knowledge of the topics involved.

Instead, citizen panels function by summoning policy and scientific experts to provide them with testimonies and vital information on the topic being discussed. The panel questions these experts, and their explanations and advice are pitted against that of experts who hold different views. In what constitutes a key part of the deliberative process, citizen panelists (assisted by trained facilitators) critically assess the evidence presented to them. Thus, the decisions they reach are based on a comprehensive, rigorous understanding of the issue(s) before them.

It's worth pointing out that, in their initial lack of knowledge and understanding of specific policy matters, members of citizen panels are not that different from our elected representatives. For any piece of legislation being considered in parliament, most of its members will not come close to being "experts" on that particular topic, either.

◆ ◆ ◆

But even if we believe that ordinary citizens have the skills required for the job, isn't it dangerous to randomly recruit the members of these citizen panels? Our first instinct is probably to draw upon our personal reservoir of prejudices and envision a panel made up of particularly unsavory characters who are handed the power to formulate and/or review public policy! How can that possibly be a good idea?[13]

Fortunately, this fear is misplaced, as simple calculations can attest. As long we accept that a substantial majority of our fellow citizens are decent, honest people, then the probability of drawing a citizen panel dominated by unsavory characters is abysmally low. Consider the hypothetical case of citizen panels made up of 24 participants. If you believe that one out of every ten people is a bad apple, then the chances of half or more of the participants in that panel being rotten are practically zero. This remains true under even more-pessimistic worldviews: for those who guess that one out of every five people (a whopping 20% of the population—reason enough to hardly ever leave home) is not to be trusted, the chance of them making up half or more of the people on that 24-seat panel remains at 0.10%.

	Majority of 50%	Supermajority of 60%	Supermajority of 70%
24 citizens†	6.77%	0.32%	0.02%
90 citizens	0.08%	~0%	~0%
160 citizens‡	~0%	~0%	~0%

The risk of bad apples taking over. Even under the radical assumption that 1/3 of citizens are not to be trusted, tweaking panel size or the majority required to pass a decision quickly reduces the probability of a panel dominated by unsavory types. †Dimension of Oregon review panels. ‡ Dimension of BC Citizens' Assembly

Better yet: we can actually make the odds of unsavory types taking control of a citizen panel as low as we wish. It

---

[13] You might notice that this section does not define who, exactly, these "unsavory" types might be. This is done on purpose. This section's argument and simple math apply regardless of the particular prejudices (or ideological preferences) of each reader.

does come at a cost, but it can be achieved in either of two different ways.

The first option is to make the panel larger. By having more citizens on the panel, the proportion of bad apples sitting on it will tend to be closer to the proportion in the general population (1/10 or 1/5, respectively, in the examples above). The fact that deliberation works best in relatively small groups (experienced facilitators say that panels shouldn't have more than 25 participants) does not pose a significant obstacle since larger panels can be—and frequently are—subdivided into multiple smaller work-groups.[14]

The second option is to increase the percentage of votes required for the panel to pass a decision. For example, if we demand a "supermajority" of at least 60% (rather than just 50% plus one vote), then the likelihood of there being enough unsavory types on the panel for them to effectively control it will also become smaller.

Taken together, these two parameters give us good reason to trust that the nightmare scenarios that we all involuntarily conjure when we think of a random grouping of our fellow citizens will stay that way—more a portrayal of our deep-seated fears about the society we live in than a situation likely to occur.

Does this mean we can be *absolutely* sure that such a system would never produce a panel dominated by people we should rightly be concerned about? No. But electoral politics likewise provides no assurances of that, as a cursory glance at twentieth-century history books will attest. (We will revisit this topic in the conclusion.)

◆ ◆ ◆

---

[14] See, for an extreme example, the several "Citizen Summits" organized by AmericaSpeaks in which thousands participated.

Exploring the implications of randomness a bit further, there are some other things we can say about the composition of citizen panels recruited in this way. In particular, we know that participants will tend to be as smart, educated and wise as the average citizen. The panels' demographic make-up will also tend to mirror that of the general population in terms of gender, age, race, occupation and socioeconomic status.[15] And the same will be true of political views and attitudes: the people who comprise citizen panels will tend to be from different political persuasions in the same proportions as we find them in the general population.

Compare this—the prospect of policy being formulated and/or reviewed by groups of citizens who mirror the make-up of the general population—with our current system. As mentioned earlier, professional politicians are very different from the rest of us in several important ways. The political class is disproportionately made up of white males from a narrow range of professional backgrounds who are significantly wealthier than the average citizen they are supposed to represent. Citizen panels, on the other hand, would constitute a true cross-section of our society. Statistically speaking, such citizen panels would be much more "representative" of the general citizenry than our elected representatives ever have been.

◆ ◆ ◆

So, where and for what purpose has citizen deliberation been used in recent times? Let's survey two different real-world cases.[16]

---

[15] A common sampling method known as stratified random sampling can be used to ensure that all panels effectively mirror the general population across such key demographic traits.

[16] Note that this is in addition to many hundreds of "citizen juries"

The first of these took place in the Canadian province of British Columbia. In 2004, the provincial government randomly recruited 160 citizens to form a "citizens' assembly," which was asked to investigate how the provincial voting system should be reformed. The government promised upfront that the assembly's proposals would be put up for a vote in a referendum and, if approved by the population, implemented.

The 2004 British Columbia Citizens' Assembly on Electoral Reform

Over the course of eleven weekends, these citizens learned about different electoral systems, consulted with experts and eventually decided to propose a voting system based largely

---

organized by governments the world over in recent decades. Such citizen juries function in a way similar to that described above, yet are typically devoid of any real political power. Instead, governments use them either as "beefed-up" focus groups (to determine which decisions might be acceptable to the public) or, at worst, to help legitimize decisions which, in fact, have already been made.

on what is known as "Single Transferable Vote" (STV).[17] Dating back to the early 19th century, STV is a well-known alternative to the two most common voting systems and is currently used for national elections in Ireland, Australia and Malta. In the words of David Farrell (professor of politics at University College Dublin), STV is the voting system that "politicians, given a choice, would probably least like to see introduced but which voters, given a choice, should choose."

When the referendum took place, the changes proposed by the citizens' assembly were approved by a majority of 57% of the population. However, the results failed to fulfill all the strict requirements the government had imposed for them to be considered binding, and, disappointingly, the reforms were never implemented.

Another famous case of citizen panels wielding real power is that of the Citizens' Initiative Review process in the US state of Oregon. Referendums have a long history in that state, dating back to 1902. More than a century later, in 2010, Oregon public officials agreed to introduce a substantial innovation in the way ballot measures are handled.

What they did was to add a deliberative "layer" to the process. Before a referendum is held, a panel of 24 randomly chosen citizens now deliberates for a number of days on the measure being proposed. After interviewing advocates on both sides and consulting scientific experts who provide them with in-depth information on the topic, these citizens carefully analyze the question before them and conclude their work by issuing a public statement.

Written in everyday language and not more than two or three pages long, this document includes the panel's key findings about the choice facing the electorate; short group

---

[17] We will revisit the topic of voting systems in the next chapter.

statements by the panelists who support and oppose the ballot measure; and any additional considerations that the panel collectively deems relevant. How many panelists support and oppose the measure at the end of the deliberation period is clearly indicated; the same information is provided for each of the panel's key findings, allowing readers to easily gauge how convincing the panel found each of them once the group had carefully researched the issue.

The full statement is then included in the "voter's pamphlet" that all registered voters in Oregon receive in the mail before a referendum. Recently conducted research by John Gastil and colleagues at Pennsylvania State University (quoted earlier) indicates that these statements not only succeed in making voters more knowledgeable about ballot measures, but also substantially influence the voting behavior of those who read them.

Members of a citizen panel in Oregon analyzing a ballot measure.

The cases of British Columbia and Oregon clearly refute the establishment's warnings of the "tremendous risks" inherent in the kind of "democratic experimentalism" advocated in this book. As these tales make clear, there is no reason to believe that bringing citizen deliberation into the core of our political systems would somehow wreak havoc on society. And I am not alone in my views. Consider, for example, that the Oregon legislature itself recently chose—after a successful one-year trial period—to pass a law making the Citizen Initiative Review a permanent feature of the way referendums are conducted in that state. All available evidence suggests that citizen deliberation is a safe and promising way to democratize our political institutions.

♦ ♦ ♦

So, how might we incorporate citizen deliberation into existing political systems? In the short-term, a reasonable goal would be to import the deliberative apparatus of the Citizen Initiative Review process found in Oregon. Later in this book, we will see how it can be fruitfully combined with referendums that increase our control over the political class. Most countries already have referendums in some form: adding a citizen review panel to the process—and ensuring that all registered voters had easy access to the panel's conclusions—would serve two important purposes. First, it would contribute to more-informed decision-making on the part of the electorate, as the evidence from Oregon shows. Second, it would help familiarize the general population with citizen deliberation, thus paving the way for its broader use.

Acquainting citizens with the process of citizen deliberation matters. It is my personal experience that, even in a context of total disillusionment with, and often outright hostility towards, the political class, citizens will be extremely skeptical of having other "ordinary people" actively engaged in politics. Those chanting in protest outside a besieged parliament might nod in agreement upon hearing a proposal to summarily jail those in power, yet will most often balk at the notion of their fellow citizens being directly involved in policy matters.

This state of affairs is sad but understandable. When it comes to politics, ordinary citizens have, for too long, been reduced to the role of mere spectators. Thus, suggesting that things could be different will inevitably seem alien to most. Combined with our tendency to harbor nearly pathological levels of distrust towards anyone outside our immediate social circle, this creates substantial challenges for anyone advocating greater citizen involvement in policy-making. (We will revisit this topic in the conclusion.)

In the long term, we should aim higher and look at some of the more ambitious proposals that have been advanced. The main idea is to have a large citizen panel—ranging in size from, say, 50 participants to the few hundreds typical of a lower house of parliament—constitute a separate legislative chamber. If this sounds strange, think for a moment about the tremendous potential demonstrated by citizen deliberation in both British Columbia and Oregon over the last decade. After giving it some thought, you might find yourself wondering instead: if *ad hoc* citizen panels work that well, why not try to tap into this source of reasoned, public-spirited decision-making on a more permanent basis? This is the rationale behind those bolder proposals.

A "citizens' chamber" would be picked at random from the general population. Its members would take a legally-protected leave from their regular jobs and receive an adequate wage for their work. Throughout their time in office, they would be assisted by staff who would not only act as facilitators, but would also support them in their various duties. Each citizens' chamber would serve a single, non-renewable term that should be sufficiently long for its members to get acquainted with their new role, but also short enough to prevent them from becoming too accustomed to the continued exercise of power.

This citizens' chamber would review the measures passed by elected representatives. With a sufficiently large supermajority, it would be able to block (or demand amendments to) the decisions made by the traditional elected chamber. In situations of irreconcilable disagreement, a deadlock would be resolved through a referendum: the public would decide which of the two chambers of parliament to side with.[18]

Obviously, any plan of this sort faces a long wait before seeing the light of day. In the meantime, we can make significant inroads by promoting the establishment of citizens' chambers at the city level. The recent popularity of participatory budgeting in cities all around the globe provides more than just grounds for optimism: it could also be used to convincingly argue that the (perceived) distance separating us from this kind of solution is not that great after all.

---

[18] For an example of a more nuanced proposal, see Terrill Bouricius' article *Democracy Through Multi-Body Sortition: Athenian Lessons for the Modern Day*.

#2 VOTING LIKE THE IRISH WHILE CAMPAIGNING LIKE THE FRENCH

With the following set of proposals, we'll shift our focus from citizen deliberation to the voting booth. Elections have been with us for a long time, yet in most countries they continue to operate in ways that are too protective of established interests. This chapter explores some ideas for how elections—despite their intrinsic limitations—might be reformed. More concretely, we will look into changes that could (i) allow voters to more fully express their preferences and (ii) make the electoral process fairer.

Voting like the Irish

For those of us who still bother to vote, an election day often forces us into a tricky situation. On the one hand, we have our actual preferences over the different candidates. On the other, there is that little voice inside our head reminding us that only one or two of them actually stand a chance of winning the majority of the votes—and we had better take that into account, or else a candidate we particularly dislike might win the election.[19]

---

[19] As will soon become clear, this section could just as easily have been entitled, "Voting like the Australians" or "Voting like the Maltese."

Thus, voting becomes a difficult exercise of trying to reconcile two different realities: our multifaceted preferences and the fact that we can tick only one box. As a result, many voters end up casting ballots for establishment candidates from a mainstream party that they do not truly support. They reason (correctly) that, by voting for a smaller party, they might be "wasting" their vote and that they'd better help elect the "least bad" of the mainstream candidates.

While arguably making a country more "governable," the fact that the larger, mainstream parties end up receiving a greater percentage of the votes also has serious negative implications. In particular, the big parties feel less threatened by elections and, thus, become even less accountable to the citizenry. At the same time, outsiders are dissuaded from launching new political projects that could challenge the status quo since they know that they stand a minimal chance of getting elected. These factors contribute to the existence of a stale, self-assured political class that knows itself to be largely untouchable.

♦ ♦ ♦

Things could be different. We could, instead, use a voting system that would allow us to more accurately express our preferences over the different candidates, while also helping to break the stranglehold that the large, established parties have on our political systems.

"Rank voting" is a simple and powerful idea. Instead of casting a vote for a single candidate, voters are asked to *order* all the candidates according to their preferences. For example, voters are able to express that they like *Small Party A* the best, that they prefer *Big Party B* over *Big Party C* and that they strongly oppose *Small Party D*. Ranking alternatives is something that is intimately familiar to most of us: the adoption of rank voting simply extends this common, everyday practice to the act of choosing who will represent us.

STV BALLOT

- Three members to be elected
- Number the boxes in the order of your choice
- Write the number "1" in one of the boxes and then show as many other preferences as you wish

Smith, Freda	APPLE PARTY	4
Gil, Steven	APPLE PARTY	1
Howard, Brenda	APPLE PARTY	2
Roberts, Saul	INDEPENDENT	3
Jansen, Doug	PEAR PARTY	6
Wong, Lisa	PEAR PARTY	
Lewis, Peter	PEAR PARTY	
Savoie, Christine	MANGO PARTY	5

Rank voting is easy: voters simply order candidates according to their preferences. (Adapted from the BC Citizens' Assembly on Electoral Reform report.)

Rank voting is, perhaps, more accurately described as a "family" of voting systems. Though the underlying idea is always the same, voting theorists have devised quite a number of variations. These variations all look alike to voters, but there can be big differences "under the hood" in terms of how individual preferences are aggregated and then used to distribute the available seats among the candidates.[20]

This book proposes the adoption of a rank voting system known as "single transferable vote" (STV). While some other good options exist, STV has two important advantages. First, it is a form of proportional representation. This means that, unlike what happens in majority ("first-past-the-pole") systems, as long as some conditions are met, then the set of representatives who get elected will closely mirror the proportion of votes cast for the different parties. Second, STV is already in use in several parts of the world. For example, it is currently employed at the national level to elect the members of the Irish and Maltese parliaments and of the Australian senate (in addition to a variety of regional and local elections around the world). Therefore, advocating its adoption should be easier since we can point to the cases of Ireland, Malta and Australia when fending off accusations of "experimentalism."

How does STV combine the preferences of individual voters to select a set of winners? The algorithm isn't trivial, but the idea behind it is easy to understand. STV works by "transferring" votes between the different candidates in such a way that (i) when a candidate stands no chance of being elected, any vote cast for her is transferred to that voter's *next* favorite candidate who has not yet secured a seat; and (ii) when a candidate has already received enough votes to be elected, any "surplus" votes she receives will likewise be transferred to the next preference of those voters. The

---

[20] It is worth keeping in mind that no voting system is perfect. In fact, it is known to be mathematically impossible for any voting system to meet all the desirable criteria that voting theorists have identified.

following analogy by Douglas J. Amy, professor of politics at Mount Holyoke College, might help clarify how this works:

> *Imagine a school where a class is trying to elect a committee. Any student who wishes to run stands at the front of the class and the other students vote for their favorite candidates by standing beside them. Students standing almost alone next to their candidate will soon discover that this person has no chance of being elected and move to another candidate of their choice to help him or her get elected. Some of the students standing next to a very popular candidate may realize that this person has more than enough support to win, and decide to go stand next to another student that they would also like to see on the committee. In the end, after all of this shuffling around, most students would be standing next to candidates that will be elected, which is the ultimate point of this process.*

♦ ♦ ♦

However, an improved voting system is not, in itself, enough to ensure better electoral representation. A variety of other (even geekier) factors should be kept in mind. An important one is how to define and allocate seats to constituencies. In particular, one needs to guard against attempts at strategic manipulation by larger parties.

The reason for this is that dominant parties will often try to use their power to redefine the boundaries of constituencies so as to make it easier for them to gain more seats in coming elections. They can accomplish this by redrawing the lines so that in each constituency: (i) the party has just enough supporters to secure a majority; and (ii) the party splits its main opponent's voter base across multiple constituencies, so that, within each constituency, that opponent no longer receives sufficient votes to win any seats.

It is also possible for the more powerful parties to "break" proportional representation by splitting the territory into a larger number of constituencies, each of them electing just a handful of seats. As the number of seats in each constituency decreases, so do the smaller parties' chances of securing any representation at all. This "trick" makes so-called "proportional representation" systems produce results that resemble those of first-past-the-post elections— thus cementing the power of the large, entrenched parties at the expense of non-establishment voices.

Campaigning like the French

Another issue central to electoral reform is that of campaign and party finance. The promiscuity between private funds and political parties is a well-known issue in almost every country. When discussing why vast sums of private money and electoral politics do not belong together, we can start by making two simple observations:

1. If we are to respect the notion that elections are about the citizenry choosing candidates based on their intrinsic merits, then it makes no sense for some to stand on a taller soapbox merely because they have privileged access to greater pools of money.

2. Even in the absence of outright corruption, the dependence of the political class on massive private donations is bound to make politicians unduly sensitive to the needs of the individuals and special interest groups who contributed to their campaigns.

Both of these premises seem straightforward.[21] However, they describe a world that is a far cry from the reality most of us live in. The reforms enacted in France between the late 1980s and the early 2000s suggest that things could be different. Over this period, that country took significant steps to curb the role of money in politics and seems to have succeeded. Without painting an excessively rosy picture—or suggesting that we should hope to ever truly separate the two—the French experience suggests that it *is* worthwhile to ask ourselves how to insulate the realm of politics from the corrupting effects of money.

Our best shot at holding fair elections is to have purely public funding of political parties and campaigns, handed out according to an equitable and democratically acceptable principle. It should be evident that private funding (regardless of whether it takes the form of donations, advertising or any other kind of paid support) is problematic. Unless you accept that catering to the interests of the wealthier segments of the population and moneyed special interest groups legitimately

---

[21] Not so in the US, though. In that country, many equate donations and other forms of paid support for political campaigns to constitutionally protected political speech. In particular, over the last four decades, the US Supreme Court has repeatedly supported the notion that constraints on money spent to promote (or attack) a political candidate are inadmissible. One can take the extent to which the US political system has been overrun by corporations and other special interest groups as at least indicative of the perils inherent in that approach. As an illustration, consider the unexpectedly candid words of Dick Durbin, a senior US senator, after the near-meltdown of the global financial system: "[T]he banks . . . are still the most powerful lobby on Capitol Hill. And they frankly own the place." Similarly, in his influential 2009 essay *The Quiet Coup*, Simon Johnson, former chief economist of the IMF, pointed out how the financial industry has effectively gained control over the US federal government and, thus, has become impervious to any kind of meaningful supervision.

entitles a candidate to be better heard at election time, then private funding should be reduced to (at most) modest individual donations.[22] Given that operating a party and running an electoral campaign costs a substantial amount of money — i.e., far more than what parties and campaigns might net from small individual donations—it will be necessary for the state to step in and finance these activities.

So, what is an "equitable and democratically acceptable" way to hand out public funds? Obviously, governments cannot unquestioningly hand out public money to anyone who announces the intention to run for office. That would not only be impracticable, but would also likely result in an indecipherable election-time cacophony. We need a "filter" of some kind. Two possibilities are:

1. giving out a flat subsidy to any party that is able to collect a required number of supporting signatures; or

2. handing out public funds in proportion to each party's performance in the last general election, with newcomers (who demonstrate having an adequate number of supporters) being awarded a more-basic subsidy.

The first rule has the advantage of coming close(r) to establishing a level playing field for all contestants, while the second introduces an element of positive feedback that can promote some stability in electoral results (admittedly at the expense of smaller parties). Both are defensible goals, with the latter system already being used in multiple countries. In either case, the required number of signatures must be

---

[22] The definition of "modest" is obviously open to debate, but it is probably a fair bet to say that this principle requires ruling out individual contributions that would represent a sizeable chunk of the disposable income of most citizens.

chosen carefully, so that spurious candidates are filtered out, while incumbents are not excessively protected from the threat of newcomers.[23]

♦ ♦ ♦

Such reforms on sources of funding, though, are only half of the picture. Equally, if not more, important is to cap campaign and party spending. There are at least two reasons for aggressively pursuing such a strategy:

1. If campaigns and parties are not allowed to spend more than the total amount they collect from public funding and small individual contributions, then their incentives for illicitly obtaining additional funds from private sources will be reduced. While clever campaign/ party operatives might still find a way to misrepresent the true origin of illegally obtained funds, most *effective* campaign spending will, by definition, be *highly visible*. (For example, according to the *New York Times*, in the 2012 US presidential campaign, "media and advertising"—neither of which can be "concealed"—accounted for half of the total expenditures by both candidates.) Radically cutting how much

---

[23] Public funding handed out according to popular support for a party/candidate also serves as the inspiration for a set of proposed reforms in the US. Acting within the strong constraints imposed by the US Supreme Court on campaign/party finance reform, Yale law professors Bruce Ackerman and Ian Ayres' idea of "patriot dollars" would endow US voters with a government "voucher" that they could distribute as they saw fit among running candidates. In his most recent book, Lawrence Lessig made a similar proposal. His "Grant and Franklin Project," named for the past US presidents whose faces appear on $50 and $100 bills, would see citizens receive a $50 or $100 tax rebate that they could use to fund political candidates or parties of their choosing.

money candidates and parties are allowed to spend will reduce the influence of money on electoral politics and, thus, help level the playing field.

2. Such a drastic reduction in funding would also necessarily alter the way political campaigns are conducted— perhaps changing the terms of political competition for the better. In their current form, electoral campaigns spend most of their resources trying to gain an advantage by means that have little to do with either reasoned, informed argument by the candidates or reasoned, informed reflection by the voters. Mass advertising, rallies at which candidates preach to the converted, and the use of political consultants to strategize ad nauseum about whom to "target" or how to tweak a candidate's "message" can hardly be seen as bringing us closer to any ideal of democratic representation.

Drastically cutting campaign spending while promoting a cost-effective—and, most importantly, "debate-improving"— transition to largely Internet-based campaigning could meaningfully change the face of electoral politics.

Although the low quality of millions of Youtube comments admittedly suggests otherwise, we can now build web-based platforms that allow a large number of people to make meaningful contributions to a discussion. Such systems could be used, for example, to gather questions and counter-arguments from the general public in response to a candidate's public statements or media appearances. Journalists, bloggers and activists would then be able to follow up on the issues identified in that way.

For example, a web platform could be devised in which each candidate would be given the opportunity to host all of his or her media content and public appearances. Citizens at large and the other candidates would be able to attach questions to—or otherwise critically engage with—each candidate's materials and public statements. Contributions made in this way would gain visibility as they got more votes from other participants in the forum. The task of moderating this forum would be delegated to a committee of representatives from all the *other* candidates running in that election. That would ensure that the questions that rise to the top—and, thus, have the best chance of spanning media coverage and debate—are not just relevant, but are those that the candidate's *opponents* would most like to see addressed. The candidate's answers to these questions would then also become available for challenge, and this cycle of public scrutiny and debate would start over again.

While I don't harbor any fantasies that information technology will magically bring about a golden age of reasoned political debate, much of what currently passes for political discourse sets such a low bar that thinking that an intelligently designed system could improve upon the present situation doesn't seem far-fetched at all. The massive electoral advertising campaigns we find in many countries do little more than bombard the public with generic messages promoting the "honesty" and "respectability" of a candidate. These campaigns work solely by appealing to either primitive forms of identification ("this is the candidate of *my* party, so I will support her") or, more perversely, by tapping into subconscious preconceived notions of what a "respectable" or "competent" politician is supposed to look like. If caps on political spending resulted in far fewer such messages, it might even happen that quite a number of voters would redirect their attention to the more reasoned content of a web platform like the one described above. And that, I would argue, could, in itself, turn out to be pretty good news.

Actually implementing voting law reforms

Wrapping up this chapter, it is important to reemphasize that the devil is in the details. Switching to a "better" voting system is meaningless if the number of seats in most constituencies is so small that the victory of the largest parties is effectively ensured. Similarly, it is also easy to leave loopholes in campaign and party finance regulation. For example, limits on campaign spending are of little use if electoral campaigns are defined as starting just a few weeks before an election, and parties are free to spend as much as they like promoting their candidates *before* the official start of the campaign.

We have to carefully address these and myriad other questions if reforms are to prove effective. In fact, this is true of *all* of the proposals presented in this book. Readers who are wisely allergic to generalities can rest assured that the challenges—and opportunities—this presents will be addressed later in the book.

#3 KEEPING A TIGHT GRIP:
THE SWISS-OREGONIAN LOCK

Now, let's turn our attention to what happens *between* elections. In particular, what might be done to keep politicians in check after we have elected them? By now, the motivation for this must be clear. From prime ministers who use false pretexts to lead a nation into war, to governments that unflinchingly implement radical and nearly-irreversible public sector "reforms" in the face of widespread public opposition, all too often we find ourselves at the mercy of those we have elected.

These kinds of actions by our elected officials raise important questions about the democratic legitimacy of much of what is done in our name. They also make it evident that we need some sort of emergency mechanism that would allow us to stop the political class from adopting measures that citizens strongly oppose.  Without the political equivalent of a bright-red "STOP" button like the ones in elevators, it will remain easy for politicians to continue abusing the power we have entrusted them with.

We can find the basic building block for such a political "panic button" in Switzerland: the citizen-initiated referendum. By gathering a sufficient number of signatures, citizens who strongly oppose a government measure are able to subject it to a popular vote.[24] Though the underlying idea is a simple one, a few considerations are in order.

First, campaigning to hold a referendum and collecting the required number of signatures is often a very costly enterprise. That means that, unless adequate measures are taken, special interest groups with access to large amounts of money will have a substantial advantage in using these referendums to advance their political agendas. Therefore, we need to ensure that such campaigns are financed exclusively through grassroots support (i.e., small individual contributions). Fortunately, and because the Internet has made raising the public's awareness of an issue and collecting signatures so much easier, imposing strict financing rules may very well level the playing field without placing an undue burden on the ability to campaign.

Second, the same logic implies that—once enough signatures have been collected and it has been determined that a referendum will indeed take place—both sides should be subject to the restrictions on funding sources we discussed earlier. In particular, both sides should receive an equal amount of public funding.

Third, it is important that the results of such a referendum be binding. Given the generally low levels of electoral turnout, referendums can easily fail to meet the 50% turnout threshold that many countries require for the results to be binding. All too often, politicians can already rest assured that their opponents in civil society will fail to meet the necessary criteria for a referendum to be held in the first

---

[24] A referendum of this kind is often called an "abrogative" referendum. As in the previous chapters, the details matter: the required number of signatures needs to simultaneously balance the conflicting needs of (i) being high enough as not to make everyday governance impossible and (ii) being low enough so that the referendum acts as an effective check on politicians.

place. What these turnout requirements do is ensure that citizens will then face yet another uphill battle not only to gain popular approval, but also to secure the required turnout for the referendum to have its intended effect.

Unless there is some indication of electoral foul play, these turnout requirements should be waived, and referendum results should be binding. In established democracies, where there are no threats or barriers to electoral participation, it is difficult to justify ignoring the outcome of a referendum simply because a majority of the population opted to stay home. Unlike what happens in general elections (where abstention is better understood as a refusal to support any of the electable candidates than as an expression of true political apathy), not voting in a referendum necessarily implies that a voter either does not particularly care about the matter at hand or judges herself unable to vote in a meaningful way. Neither of those seems a valid reason to ignore the preferences of those who opted to vote.

◆ ◆ ◆

Yet referendums suffer from the well-known problems we discussed earlier. In particular, voters typically come to the voting booth without adequate information and having done little to no serious reflection on the choice(s) facing them. The results can be seen in referendum-happy California, where a series of decisions made over the years in referendums have contributed to making that American state close to ungovernable. Without modifications, referendums provide a way for the popular voice to make itself heard over that of the political class; unfortunately, we cannot assume that the citizens will speak in a *reasoned, informed* way. This warrants two considerations.

First, recall a remedy for this problem that we looked at earlier: these binding referendums on the politicians' decisions should be modeled after Oregon's Citizen Initiative Review. After the required signatures have been collected, a randomly appointed citizen panel would convene to deliberate, with the input of experts and advocates, on the topic at hand. This citizen panel would then produce a statement that would serve as a reliable, trustworthy source of information for the electorate. Media coverage would ensure that voters would have easy access to the panel's views and conclusions before the referendum.[25]

Second, the same general concerns suggest that it might be wise to use referendums strictly as a way for the electorate to pass judgment on the decisions politicians make. Enabling groups of citizens to actively *propose* new laws that would come into force if approved in a popular vote seems a dangerous proposal. The case of California warrants this concern, as does the recent use of popular initiatives in Switzerland to advance openly xenophobic agendas. Adding an Oregon-style citizen deliberation layer to the process should help us mitigate the risk of unreasoned, emotional popular decisions at the ballot box. However, it makes sense to err on the side of caution and stick to the initially stated goal of merely *curbing the power of politicians*. As we have seen, the best tool for achieving this is a citizen-initiated

---

[25] Ensuring that all of the media would play a constructive role in this process could be done by legally mandating the publication/ broadcasting of the panel's recommendations and also by protecting the panel's right of reply. Though a far cry from addressing the broader issue of what is the proper role of the media in a democratic society, this should at least help mitigate the risk that these measures would end up further empowering those groups that already enjoy a privileged relationship with mainstream media outlets.

referendum that gives citizens a chance to revoke decisions made by politicians—and that is exclusively what I am advocating in this chapter.

◆ ◆ ◆

It could also be worthwhile to endow these referendums with sharper political teeth. While the actions of some politicians might simply be misguided, there is other, far more egregious behavior to be concerned about. For example, some politicians may actively try to deceive the public so that they can better serve private interests. Or they might act in a way that clearly goes against the platform or major promises on which they were elected.

Such extreme circumstances warrant the voters' ability not merely to *reverse* the decisions made by politicians, but also to effectively punish them for their actions. We can find a model for how to do this in recall elections, which already exist in a number of US states and Swiss cantons (in addition to several other parts of the world). As their name suggests, these are elections in which the public decides whether an elected politician should be ousted from office.

One way to make referendums more effective tools of citizen control would be to give them a similar "recall option." For example, when participating in a referendum, citizens could face three different choices:

• They could *support* the measure being challenged in the referendum, thus "agreeing" with the politicians who implemented/approved it.
• They could vote to *repeal* it, while believing that the politician or group of politicians who supported it, though mistaken, acted in reasonably good faith.

• They could vote to repeal it *and* to oust the politicians who promoted it, judging that a serious breach of trust had occurred.

To help voters reach a more reasoned view on whether a recall might be warranted, the citizen panel would also deliberate on this matter.

◆ ◆ ◆

Among the measures advocated in this book, promoting a more effective mechanism for citizens to check the actions of the political class may be the most appealing to the general population. By having a citizen panel reflect and share its views on the matter up for referendum—as is done in Oregon's Citizen Initiative Review process—this reform can be an important step towards acquainting the public with the virtues of citizen deliberation. Thus, by exploiting the populist appeal of, quite literally, "kicking a politician out of office," we will not just bring greater accountability into our political system—we will also be planting the seeds for a more deliberative future.

#4 LEARNING FROM THE BRITISH TABLOID PRESS

There are a number of ways in which the hands of the political class are said to be tied. Perhaps the main one is our membership in international—or "supranational"—institutions such as the European Union (EU). Though the following discussion will use the EU as an example, the points I will make apply equally to other ambitious political integration projects occurring in other parts of the globe. There seems to be an unswerving enthusiasm among the international political class for dividing the world into a handful of large regional blocks, as evidenced by all the effort invested in the establishment of the Union of South American Nations and the African Union.

These regional blocks serve many useful purposes. The abolition of internal borders facilitates trade and the free movement of individuals. Their institutions 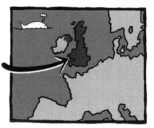 promise to act as a safety net against particularly egregious abuses by national governments. Their larger dimension also gives their members a better chance of making themselves heard in global forums. Among other advantages, this could make taking collective action on environmental and other regulatory matters substantially easier.

Yet—and as the case of the EU makes clear—this sort of integration also has other implications. They seem evident to most Europeans, but, strangely, only the parties on the fringes of the political spectrum dare point them out. Simply put, the process of integration has a huge cost in terms of the loss of political power by citizens. The more "integration" takes place, the more powerless they become. Decisions are increasingly made at the EU level—far removed from any form of democratic accountability, even by the shabby standards of national representative democracies.

Although this is a common-sense observation, it falls outside the realm of "reasonable" political debate in EU nations—with the notable exception of Britain.[26] If this is to change, we first have to distinguish between the multiple issues at play when we speak of how political integration threatens our democracies. Only then will we be able to have a meaningful debate about the participation of our countries in international projects of this kind.

♦ ♦ ♦

Looking at the case of Europe, a part of the problem is the multiple layers of *un*accountability separating the top echelons of the EU leadership from the European citizenry.

---

[26] British readers might laugh off the notion of this being an admirable aspect of their political reality. While the title of this chapter is admittedly little more than a provocation, the truth remains that, in Britain, it is acceptable to openly discuss the country's membership in the EU. Contrast that with the situation in the rest of Europe. For several years now, many millions of Europeans—all the way from the creditor nations in the north to the indebted south—have been wondering when, exactly, they signed up for the rollercoaster ride that their EU membership has turned into. Yet, in most of their countries, you would be hard-pressed to find more than a vestige of euroscepticism in mainstream political discourse.

The European Council is composed mainly of national heads of state or government, who are already largely unaccountable in their home countries and who become *even more so* in the context of the European Council. When they meet in Brussels, their detachment from the populations they are meant to serve becomes even greater. Not only are they operating in an environment that is far removed from the national democratic institutions they are nominally accountable to, but, upon returning to their home countries, they can always claim that Brussels "forced" them to implement any measure that proves especially unpopular.

The situation with the European Commission is not significantly better, either, since its members are appointed by national governments. While an incoming commission is subject, *as a whole,* to the approval of the European Parliament, its composition is ultimately the result of negotiations between national governments and the leadership of the main political groups in the European Parliament. What this means is that the top levels of the EU hierarchy are little more than extensions of our only-very-indirectly-accountable national governments.

Note that these are *design choices*: a supranational institution like the EU *need not* be so flagrantly undemocratic. It *need not* have these multiple layers shielding the higher levels of its decision-making hierarchy from public oversight. We could have more-accountable, democratic supranational institutions: the ones we currently have merely mirror back to us, in an amplified manner, the undemocratic nature of our own domestic political culture(s).

◆ ◆ ◆

Other problems, however, are unavoidable consequences of political integration. These are serious, inescapable limitations that are inherent in any larger, supranational political union.

Though often delusional in their news coverage, British tabloids ensure that the loss of sovereignty remains a frequent discussion topic in the UK.

The first of these is the centralization of decision-making. Once a central governing body of some sort is established, it will tend to accumulate power. This means that decisions that should have been made *locally* increasingly end up being made centrally. Put bluntly, citizens are no longer free to decide how they want to do things in their own countries.

As one might expect, this process generates one-size-fits-all decisions that often fail to take into account the needs and issues specific to each nation.

A second, distinct issue is that centralization (further) insulates politicians from the citizens they represent. The greater the geographical and administrative distance separating them, the more difficult it becomes for politicians to be sensitive to citizens' concerns. The situation grows even worse as politicians spend an increasing amount of their time in international high-level summits, where they deal only with other foreign leaders—themselves also far-removed from those they represent. A world in which important decisions are increasingly made in settings of this kind is one in which we will all become more and more disempowered.

Third, centralization radically impacts the (relative) ability of different groups to influence public policy. The more centralized and, thus, more distant the political decision-making, the more asymmetric access to those decision-makers will become. For example, large corporations, international institutions and, perhaps, a few well-funded NGOs can afford to send countless lobbyists to Brussels to influence the decisions being made there. Citizen movements, unions and grassroots activists, on the other hand, will never be able to make themselves heard in a similar way. Large-scale street protests cannot happen when people need to fly, drive or walk thousands of kilometers to show their anger outside the doors of those in power. Centralization effectively means that the only way to be reliably heard is to hire professional lobbyists to represent you where the decisions are being made. That ensures that the voice of powerful special interest groups will always be heard loud and clear, while that of the citizenry will remain safely inaudible.

♦ ♦ ♦

With this said, the fact remains that supranational institutions serve a number of important functions. Careful balancing of the clear costs of political integration, on the one hand, and the reality of our need for international cooperation, on the other, is, therefore, in order.

Finding that balance, though, is very different from the unquestioningly pro-integration stance of the political class that rules most of our countries. This chapter advocates that, like the British, we must be willing to reevaluate our international commitments. After all, we citizens have the ultimate say on what our "international obligations"—that beloved scapegoat of our unaccountable leaders—really are.

♦ ♦ ♦

While Britain's *willingness* to rethink its EU membership is an example to follow, its approach is less so. With a handful of tabloids and opportunistic politicians largely setting the tone of the "debate" on this contentious matter, holding a traditional referendum seems a poor choice. Clearly, some other tool is needed when collectively deciding on issues that can have such far-ranging implications. That is what we turn our attention to in the next chapter.

#5 RECOVERING OUR DISTANCE VISION IN SAINT PETERSBURG

The plan called for it to be built on the shores of the Neva. It would consist of four large geometric structures made of glass and held together by a helicoidal metal structure, and it would serve as both a monument to the Bolshevik revolution and the headquarters of the Comintern. At a height of 400 meters, it would reign over the skyline of Saint Petersburg.

The huge tower proposed by Vladimir Tatlin in 1919 was never constructed. However, through his design, a crucial idea about politics—one that is all-too-easily forgotten in our day and age—lives on.

Tatlin envisioned that the four different structures in the tower would rotate *at different speeds*. The large cylinder at the bottom would take one full year to complete a rotation. The pyramid immediately above it would move more quickly: after one month, it would again be in its original position. The second cylinder on top of the pyramid:

just one day per revolution. And, finally, at the very top of the structure: a half-sphere that completes a full rotation in just one hour.

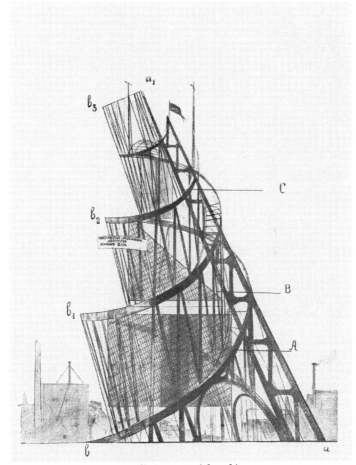

Tatlin's tower (sketch)

Since the tower was proposed not just as a monument, but also as the headquarters of the Third International, one might wonder which uses Tatlin had envisioned for each of the different parts of this imposing structure. According to his proposal, the large cylinder at the bottom rotating very slowly would house the legislature. The pyramid above it, moving faster: the executive branch. The second cylinder, which would turn even faster: a press bureau. And, finally, the half-sphere at the very top, moving faster than all the others: a radio station broadcasting news and propaganda.

◆ ◆ ◆

Tatlin's tower points the way towards the fifth measure advocated in this book. To successfully advance the public interest, a political system will need to recognize—and incorporate into its structure—the fundamental realization embodied in Tatlin's design: the need for different temporalities to coexist in the world of politics. Without this recognition, we are condemned to forever confuse our short- and long-term interests.

This issue deserves special attention because we are, both at the individual level and as a society, terrible at checking our short-term urges and acting in our own long-term interest. We know from research in psychology and behavioral economics how aggressively we tend to "discount" outcomes far in the future. This means that we give much less importance to events that will happen in the distant (or not-so-distant) future than to events that will happen soon. For example, the threat of catching a cold today might be enough to prevent us from greeting a sneezing friend with a peck on the cheek, while, at the same time, the threat of a slow death many years into the future deters comparably few smokers.

In the realm of politics, the situation is even worse. Electoral considerations and the 24-hour news cycle cultivate an even more extreme short-term orientation in our politicians. Combined with our natural tendency to be myopic decision-makers, we shouldn't be surprised when politicians appear constitutionally unable to consider the long-term implications of their decisions. As a society, we seem condemned to live in the dizzyingly fast-paced half-sphere at the top of Tatlin's tower.

♦ ♦ ♦

Some argue that we live in a "global," "interconnected," and "fast-paced" world in which "speed" and "adaptability" are the name of the game. We need even faster decision-making and a shorter reaction time on the part of the government and other public institutions—or so they tell us. This chapter makes the opposite argument—namely, that what we cannot afford are the risks of continuing with our present system. This becomes evident to anyone who pauses to really think about the issue of long-term viability in almost any domain of human endeavor. For example, only through a form of mass delusion could we believe that our political system is adequately handling concrete, large-scale systemic threats such as climate change and the fragility of the financial system.

The situation seems even more daunting when we consider looming structural challenges. We have organized society in such a way that steadily-increasing consumption is necessary to maintain a general sense of prosperity. Whenever consumption falters, our leaders are quick to shore it up by creating debt, so that demand is revived and the show can go on. That debt, however, will eventually need to be repaid. When that happens, less income will be available for consumption, and we'll find ourselves back at square one. If we step off the treadmill for a moment, we see that this cycle of increasing consumption and accumulating debt is impossible to sustain.

It takes little more than "hard, simple thinking" (as Nobel-prize-winning economist Gunnar Myrdal put it) to conclude that, on a planet with finite resources, ever-increasing consumption threatens us with environmental collapse. Not much more effort is involved in understanding the issues caused by a gigantic mountain of debt. In May 2013, the *Wall Street Journal* reported that the total world debt load stood at 313% of the global GDP. In other words, we collectively owe each other more than three times the yearly economic output of the whole planet. This makes our global economy uniquely fragile: all it takes is for an important institution to become insolvent, and we risk that the entire house of cards will come tumbling down.

Yet, as a species, we continue merrily walking down this path seeking forever-increasing economic growth—effectively betting the house on the hope that major, currently unforeseeable technological advances will end up making it all ok. We might feel sorry for (yet another generation of) young smokers who confidently tell us: "By the time I get sick from smoking, medicine will have found a cure for whatever ails me." And yet, as a society, we continue behaving in a similar, scarily myopic way. As Brian Eno put it in an essay about our dangerous focus on what he calls the "short now":

> *It's ironic that, at a time when humankind is at a peak of its technical powers, able to create huge global changes that will echo down the centuries, most of our social systems seem geared to increasingly short nows. Huge industries feel pressure to plan for the bottom line and the next shareholders meeting. Politicians feel forced to perform for the next election or opinion poll. The media attract bigger audiences by spurring instant and heated*

reactions to human interest stories while over-looking longer-term issues—[which are] the real human interest.

♦ ♦ ♦

Deviating from this path requires a more-structured, more-disciplined approach than electoral politics seems able to deliver.

With this in mind, this chapter proposes that we explicitly incorporate into our political systems mechanisms that enable long-term thinking on key topics. That would help mitigate our innate tendency to be shortsighted and reduce the risk that the latter will drive us to extinction through environmental, economic and/or social folly. One way to accomplish this is to try to decouple the everyday management of the polity from the expression of our collective long-term vision for its future.

♦ ♦ ♦

Most of us would agree that *having a plan* is useful in life. Though, over time, this plan might change a lot, it nonetheless provides some general orientation of where we want to head in the long term. Amazingly, when it comes to politics, we seem to have forgotten this basic point. Most of our politicians focus more on reacting to events in a way that preserves their chances of reelection than on trying to bring about a particular vision of how our future should look.

In those rare instances in which a government actually changes things for the better, adversarial electoral politics makes it likely that the next executive will undo at least part of those reforms. Nothing in our institutions allows for a sense of continuity that reaches *beyond* the current electoral cycle. Whatever is accomplished now will be up for rene-gotiation once the next election arrives—even if the intrinsic desirability of those measures remains unchanged. If an individual were to behave in a similarly erratic way, most of us would (rightly) fear for him.

In the wake of his country's financial collapse and at a time of national self-questioning, the Icelandic entrepreneur Guðjón Már Guðjónsson remarked that it struck him as odd that the multinational General Electric had a "vision statement" while his native country did not.[27] I would argue that we need to similarly define a long-term vision for our nations.

Armed with such a vision, we will be able to evaluate the political "managers" we elect based on the extent to which they bring our nation closer to achieving its vision. At the same time, having such a vision clearly laid out would help prevent elected officials—once in office and nearly untouch-able by the populace—from fraudulently claiming that they have a mandate to commit the entire nation to major projects that are inherently difficult to reverse (public infrastructure, energy policy and efforts to dismantle parts of the state come to mind as examples).

♦ ♦ ♦

How could such a vision be collectively generated? Here, too, citizen deliberation might prove useful. The available evidence suggests that panels of citizen deliberators are *better* at thinking about the long-term consequences of policy choices than are professional politicians constrained by short-term electoral goals and liable to be influenced by (among others) corporate interests.[28]

---

[27] GE has roughly the same number of employees as Iceland has inhabitants.

[28] The latter matters because, as briefly touched upon in our earlier

After a study of citizen panels tasked with reflecting on GMO policy, John Dryzek concluded that "the common story" that emerges is that of "reflective publics [being] much more precautionary than policy-making elites." James Fishkin observed similar results; for example, studying multiple citizen panels that gathered to discuss energy policy, Fishkin found that participants became consistently more willing to pay higher utility bills *today* to support the use of renewable energy sources (whose environmental payoff will be felt only in the medium or long term). And, in what is arguably yet another manifestation of a similar change in attitudes, political scientist Adolf Gundersen found that, through a process he termed "deliberative interviews," citizens became consistently more committed to environmental values. Thus, it seems that ordinary citizens, reasoning together, have the ability to overcome the short-term orientation that plagues so much of our political reality: they become more cautious when it comes to incurring risks and more willing to trade off comfort today for long(er)-term goals.

◆ ◆ ◆

A "Long Now Citizens' Assembly" would be a large citizen panel that would convene every ten years.[29] These citizens would be tasked with defining a national vision for the polity. They would be free from electoral pressures, and the decade between meetings would make it unambiguously clear that the panel exists in a different temporal plane from that of electoral politics.

---

discussion of delegation, the corporate world itself needs to come to grips with "short-termism." Shortsighted corporate managers will advocate any measure that might increase their short-term profits, even if doing so substantially increases the odds of bringing about the demise of their entire industry.

[29] The inspiration for this name is drawn from the Long Now Foundation, whose goal is to foster long-term thinking.

They would focus strictly on the big debates in which long-term choices need to (or can reasonably) be made. As of 2014, in several nations, these choices would likely include: the role of the state in the provision of healthcare, education and other social services; guidelines for energy and environmental policy; how to deal with immigration; terms of membership in different international organizations (as discussed in the preceding chapter); and broad principles of economic regulation. However, the citizen assembly would define its own agenda and would be unconstrained (within its broad constitutional mandate) to choose the topics it would address.[30]

It is likely that such an assembly would subdivide into different workgroups (or committees) that would then analyze these issues in greater depth. Reflecting the breadth and complexity of the questions at hand, the citizens who were randomly selected to be part of this assembly would also be appointed for longer periods—perhaps in the range of a few months.

As the end of its deliberation period approached, the assembly would focus on generating a vision statement that could garner the support of a supermajority of its members. The resulting document would then be submitted for public approval through a referendum. Their task completed, the assembly would disband, and the citizens would be discharged from their duties.

Subsequent Long Now Citizens' Assemblies would be tasked with updating or refining the vision produced by their earlier incarnations. They might find that, after ten years, some lessons have been learned, and, thus, corrections

---

[30] A somewhat related idea can be found in the writings of Thomas Jefferson, who argued for periodic constitutional conventions so that citizens would be able to collectively question—and, if deemed necessary, revise—the fundamental principles governing their society.

are necessary. Or new major issues that require long-term choices might have come into the spotlight. For example, in the wake of the ongoing financial crisis, a Long Now Citizens' Assembly held in 2015 might focus on the role of the financial sector in our societies—a topic that would most likely not have been central at the 2005 assembly.

If approved by the citizens in a referendum, the Long Now Citizens' Assembly's vision statement would become something akin to a "contract" between the citizenry and its political officials. It would offer binding, if general, guidance on how politicians should conduct public affairs. Deliberative referendums (discussed in the third chapter) would provide citizens with a powerful corrective mechanism should political officials start to deviate from this long-term vision. In the face of a government seemingly intent on contradicting this long-term vision, gathering a sufficient number of signatures would trigger a deliberative referendum on the issue. A citizen panel would be convened and, after an adequate period of study, would issue a statement on whether or not it deemed the government's actions to be in line with the long-term vision for the country. Informed by the citizen panel's statement, the public would then have the final say at the voting booth.

◆ ◆ ◆

Used in this way, citizen deliberation offers us a promising alternative vision of what a "post-ideological" political reality might be like. It allows us to progress beyond the stale, self-serving notions that term has traditionally stood for. For example, when Daniel Bell or Francis Fukuyama speak of a post-ideological world, they mean a world in which *one* ideology (which they happen to agree with) reigns unchallenged. We can do better than that.

Contemplating citizen deliberation as a mechanism to address big, long-term policy choices, we can *see through* the concept of ideology. We realize that an ideology is little more than a ready-made "bundle" of political ideals, offering a convenient, heavily-simplified vision for our future. For example, a "liberal" is a person who wants to live in a society governed by principles A and B, just as a "conservative" is someone who longs for a future shaped by values C and D. Presently, when asked to choose in which kind of world we want to live, we merely get to pick one of these pre-defined ideological labels—and the "bundle" of values that go with it. All other combinations—just like any hope of a more nuanced view of what our future should look like—seem to be off-limits.

Like a children's menu at a restaurant, ideologies implicitly assume a passive, unthinking citizenry. They are necessary in a world in which citizens can handle only a reduced set of choices and cannot be trusted to actually think about which kind of society they want to live in.

Using citizen assemblies to agree on a "national vision," on the other hand, presents us with a scenario in which the only overarching "ideal" is one of reasoned decision-making via careful, shared consideration of the most important issues facing us. Political labels fade away, ceding ground to well-reasoned and truly democratic pragmatism. And that, I would argue, is what "post-ideological" should actually mean.

CONCLUSION

> *Until now we have had such a low level of democracy, that it is about time we try something else.* — Jón Trausti Reynisson, editor-in-chief of the Icelandic daily *Dagbladid & Visir*, interviewed in 2011

In 2008, Iceland found itself in a dire situation. Its banking sector, which had been too eager to participate in the global debt folly and other forms of "financial innovation," collapsed and threatened to force Iceland into national bankruptcy. Financial chaos ensued, and the country is, to this day, still recovering from the resulting economic crisis.

Over this period, Icelanders took to the streets and, eventually, the government fell. Along the way, however, something more curious happened. The protests did not culminate merely in the resignation of Prime Minister Geir Haarde and the scheduling of a new election (two achievements that, alone, would have constituted a surprising feat of political accountability in most "democratic" nations).

Instead, Icelanders started a process of deep political renewal. By taking a random sample representative of the whole population, a "national forum" was appointed in 2010. Its approximately 1000 members—all of them "ordinary Icelanders"—were tasked with identifying the values and principles that should guide a revision of the country's constitution. A council of 25 directly-elected citizens then took these ideas as a basis and put together a first draft for a new constitution. In late 2012, in what might have been a momentous step towards Icelanders regaining control of their country, these constitutional changes were approved by a large margin in a referendum.

In parallel, Icelandic civil society launched a number of initiatives. Well aware of the key role that watchful media organizations can play in avoiding the kind of systemic institutional failure that ultimately destroyed the country's economy, a group of citizens started the Icelandic Modern Media Initiative (IMMI). Interested in fostering fearless watchdog journalism, the IMMI campaigned for a strong legal framework protecting press freedoms. Other parts of Icelandic society joined efforts in projects such as the "Ministry of Ideas," the goal of which was to provide an open platform for citizens to propose and discuss innovative ideas that could help the country climb its way back up.

However, this story serves as both a motivational and a cautionary tale. Since these developments, the Icelandic political class has succeeded in effectively killing the effort to change the constitution. Furthermore, and in yet another powerful testament to the hopelessness of electoral politics, a general election in 2013 brought back into power the same two parties whose policies had set the stage for the meltdown of the country's economy. Thus, any progress made in curbing the power of the political and economic elites looks likely to unravel.

Nevertheless, it remains true that Icelanders succeeded in doing something amazing: they launched an ambitious, wide-ranging national renewal project *of some sort*. And—as the often-rosy international media coverage of the Icelandic "revolution" has evidenced over these last few years—this is something many have long been thirsting for. Rather than demanding a simpler narrative, I would propose that we instead embrace the notion of an "Icelandic moment" in all its bittersweet richness. It conveniently encapsulates the hopes and perils inherent in any project of this nature.

◆ ◆ ◆

And this points the way to the most important battle ahead of us. The success of any effort to reform our democracies ultimately hinges on this delicate balance between dreams and (perceived) obstacles. Given the levels of public exasperation at—and hostility towards—politicians, unlike most campaigners, we do not need to concern ourselves with "raising public awareness" of these issues. The public *already* thinks that politicians don't truly represent its interests. Instead, what we need to focus on is managing the fears triggered by the thought of substantial political reform. More concretely, we need to combat the two different obstacles that pessimism puts in the way of democratic change.

◆ ◆ ◆

The first of these obstacles is the view that today's world, with all its "complexities" and "interconnectedness," makes it impossible to implement ambitious reforms that would go against the interests of the political-economic elite that rules us. Stressing the complex web of "international obligations" and the ominous threat of markets "punishing" political measures they "disapprove" of, those defending the status quo will be sure to point out just how immutable reality is.

The misleading logic supporting this argument is easy to dispense with. A useful first step is to calibrate our sense of what is possible. History is filled with examples of ambitious political reform efforts succeeding in the face of opposition much harsher than the "international obligations" and wrathful markets mentioned above. Even in light of the increasingly militarized way in which the police have been responding to protests, in most of the West, the prospect of systematic state repression against nonviolent reformers remains distant—and we should not discount the significance of this fact. A short refresher course on European 20th-century history (or a glance at the world news) is enough to establish that as a reasonable gauge for measuring just how "impossible" political change might be.

So, if violence is not the means, how does the political establishment defend itself in mature democracies such as those in the West? By having its official and unofficial spokespersons (the latter often appearing in the media as political commentators or economic experts) cultivate this idea of the international economic and political system being "too complex" to allow change to successfully take place.

The first key thing to understand is that this (at least in its undeveloped and, by far, most common form) does not even amount to a proper argument. It is an example of circular reasoning: essentially, we are being told that "changing the system is impossible because the system is unchangeable." It is more accurately described as an unsubstantiated expression of pessimism than as an argument for the difficulty of achieving change.

Second, we have to ask ourselves what it means to say that the world is "complex." A complex system is made up of many different, highly interdependent components. This means that the operation of most individual components depends on the correct functioning of a number of other components. We see this every day in many small and big ways: for example, the arrival on our dinner table of even the most common food items is the outcome of a long process involving hundreds of individuals and organizations. In this sense, our world is, indeed, complex.[31]

But let us look a little more closely at this notion. A corollary of the complexity of a system is that the complicated feedback mechanisms tying together its multiple components make the overall behavior of the system very hard to predict. This is clearly at odds with the message of the "complexity pessimists," who want us to believe that if established interests are challenged, our complex world will definitely react in a severe, punishing way. If anything, complexity implies the opposite—that we cannot reasonably expect to know how the system will react. Obviously, this is even truer in the case of social systems made up of humans and organizations.

Thus, complexity cannot be used to argue that a system is "unchangeable"—but it *can* be used to argue that we cannot know for sure how a change to one part of the system will affect the functioning of some of its other components. This is a valid concern that we will return to later.

We should also consider other ways in which our world and, in particular, our interconnected economies are commonly said to be "complex." One of them is that markets "magically" succeed in coordinating and matching the production and consumption of an almost infinite number of products and services. It is certainly an awe-inspiring process, but its most important characteristic is not its "complexity": instead, it is its *robustness*.

Network engineers will tell you that the Internet "routes around damage"—meaning that, if an important router goes down, Internet traffic that would have passed through it is automatically redirected to use a different path to reach its

---

[31] For an illustration, see the chapter in *The Pleasures and Sorrows of Work* in which Alain de Botton shadows a tuna from the Indic Ocean to a British supermarket.

destination. In a similar way, our market economies exhibit a remarkable degree of adaptability in their behavior.[32] Take an extreme example. If—because of either general political uncertainty or the adoption of particularly strict regulations—some companies decide to stop operating in a given country, the relative scarcity of the products or services those companies used to provide will lead to an increase in their price until *other* companies that are well-positioned to provide those products or services enter that market because of the increased opportunity for profit. Because managers and entrepreneurs differ both in their judgment of situations and their appetite for risk-taking, what some regard as a less attractive business climate, others will invariably see as offering unexplored business opportunities. This is the very essence of how a market economy operates, and it makes the economy robust to any sort of political change.

This is *not*, of course, to say that an economy will be unaffected by an increase in the perceived cost of (or uncertainty associated with) conducting business there. Adjustments are likely to occur and, depending on the situation, the result might well be lower output or higher prices. However, this is a far cry from the apocalyptic scenarios described by complexity pessimists. In reality, the actual "mechanics" of a market economy—which these pessimists often claim to have an expert understanding of—*ensure* that the economy will adjust to the new political and regulatory environment. Those adjustments might, on occasion, entail losses of some sort: for example, as a result of more-stringent environmental regulation, a company might decide to close down its most polluting factory, thus leading to the loss of a number of jobs. What is

---

[32] The obvious, pathological exception is the financial sector. Then again, this shouldn't be surprising: the way it currently operates—as well as the purposes it serves—has very little to do with the real economy.

important is for us to understand that, in a properly functioning democracy, any foreseeable economic adjustment of this sort is just one of the myriad of factors to be taken into account when balancing the pros and cons of a policy measure. It is *not*, as the complexity pessimists would have us believe, some sort of divine punishment for having dared to go against the "complex," "unchangeable" status quo.

No one is claiming that there will be no difficult choices to be made once our political systems become more democratic. If anything, the *opposite* will be true. Empowering the citizenry will pierce the veil of deception that our political class has so often thrown over important issues. We will be forced to confront reality—which may come as a shock—and make decisions, fully aware of their true economic, social and environmental costs. While that will undoubtedly be hard, the good news is that the economy will always adapt to the choices we make. That is simply the way market economies work.

In sum, there is no "tension" between the exercise of political freedom and the (vitality of our) economy. Such a tension only *appears* to exist to a very small, but highly influential, group: those who believe that maximum economic output should be a nation's primary objective. For them, politics is a relatively simple affair: governing well is an issue of avoiding any decisions that would harm GDP growth. Unsurprisingly, one who embraces this view easily arrives at the conclusion that a tame, oligarchic "managed democracy" is preferable to a political system in which the popular will *could* conceivably get in the way of single-mindedly maximizing GDP growth.[33]

---

[33] "Managed democracy" was the term coined by political scientist Sheldon Wolin to describe regimes that are formally democratic but where the ruling elite has learned how to perfectly manage, to its own advantage, the political and (especially) electoral processes.

However, for anyone who does *not* subscribe to this radical vision, no such tension between democracy and the economy exists at all. The economy is not the enemy of—nor is it threatened by—our exercise of political freedom. Rather than magically floating in the apolitical vacuum contrived by the authors of economics textbooks, the economy exists and operates within the bounds that the laws of physics, social norms (customs) and state regulation impose on it. And it adapts accordingly.

However, there is one way in which the global economy *can* get in the way of democratic reform within a nation or seriously impede the functioning of a more democratic government. That is through dependence on international capital markets. As of 2014, it should be evident to anyone who is aware of the sovereign debt crisis in Europe and the US congressional gridlock over the federal debt ceiling just how constraining the dependence on capital markets can be. National governments that rely on international creditors to finance their day-to-day operations are in an extremely fragile position. When, by joining a monetary union like the Euro or through self-imposed legal or constitutional constraints on their central banks, these countries tie their own hands and make debt monetization totally off-limits, they are effectively at the mercy of private creditors.

This is a constraint that cannot be "reasoned away," for it is real. In most countries, our irresponsible ruling class has created this situation, which, if left unchecked, will have our countries servicing huge public debts into perpetuity, to the benefit of bankers and their friends. The result is that we are all shackled to the international financial markets. There are

---

Thus, those in power—and the interests they represent—are able to continue implementing their favored policies, effectively unimpeded by democratic constraints. A closely related notion can be found in Colin Crouch's discussion of a post-democratic society.

various routes to a more democratic future, but they all involve eventually ending—or at least vastly reducing—this dependence. Different countries will take different paths: some will use budget surpluses to pay back their debts, while others will renege on at least some of their debt.[34] Whichever path we choose, it is important that, once we have achieved independence from international credit markets, we preserve that independence through (cyclically) balanced public budgets, "safe" use of public debt (for example, issuing debt primarily to domestic creditors and to finance specific public projects, as opposed to using it to finance the day-to-day operations of the state), and retaining the option of having the central bank monetize deficits under clear, well-defined circumstances.[35]

◆ ◆ ◆

When talking to those who view the chances of reform as virtually nil, it is worth pointing out how *mutually reinforcing* the different forms of democratic empowerment suggested in this book would be.

If, for example, we succeed in adopting a better electoral system, then this would make it easier to elect politicians

---

[34] Unlike what some market fundamentalists would like us to believe, the latter does not ensure that a nation will be teleported back to the Stone Age.

[35] It is worth pointing out that a "balanced public budget" is, at its root, not far from being a politically neutral term. It merely means that public revenue should match public spending over the same time period. In common debate, however, this term has been appropriated by those who mostly argue for the need for severe cuts in public spending. It is helpful to remember that the move towards a balanced budget can also be made through increases in public revenue—e.g., through more-aggressive taxation of corporate profits and financial trading operations, both of which currently benefit from sophisticated tax-avoidance schemes.

who would support citizen deliberation as a way to further democratize governance. Using a ranked voting system would ensure that a minority party campaigning purely on issues of political reform would have a chance of receiving substantial support since voters would not need to engage in tactical voting, for fear that the "wrong" mainstream party might get elected should they cast a vote for that minority party.

Similarly, a successful campaign to raise awareness that our "international commitments" are not set in stone but, rather, are something that a nation's citizens can collectively decide to review would make clear that social, economic and political reality *is* fundamentally in our hands and that we stand to benefit greatly from regaining control of our own *domestic* political systems. The resulting feeling of being in control would foster further citizen empowerment through greater use of citizen deliberation and/or improvements in political representation.

Finally, the adoption of citizen deliberation would obviously open the door for us to further regain control of the political system. Citizen panels could directly address the question of how to reform our electoral system and allow for serious reflection on the extent to which our participation in supranational institutions might be costing us our sovereignty.

♦ ♦ ♦

A different form of pessimism—let's call it "people pessimism"—lies behind the second, and probably more dangerous, enemy to the ideas presented in this book. It does not involve the "complex world" thinking described above. Rather, it is the far more insidious view that democratic change is undesirable because *people are stupid and/or untrustworthy*. Fighting this kind of thinking will be more difficult, for it hinges *not* on a negative view of how the world works (which can, to a reasonable extent, be meaningfully debated and disproved) but, instead, on life-long, deeply held and somewhat murky beliefs about "human nature" and whether or not "people are just stupid." Indeed, defenders of the status quo will view proposals for change as dangerous because, in their eyes, anyone crazy enough to advocate more-participatory forms of democracy is necessarily overestimating the abilities and/or intrinsic goodness of people.

Better keep them outside. The 24 randomly chosen members of an Oregon CIR panel standing on the steps of the Oregon legislature.

We should start by noting that any project to effectively return power to citizens will face this kind of criticism, but it will be especially felt when advocating citizen deliberation. Many will feel scared by the idea that "ordinary people" will be empowered and actively involved in making political decisions. Are they smart and educated enough? And, perhaps more importantly, are they to be trusted? Unfortunately, many people, upon first hearing of these ideas, will answer at least one of these two questions in the negative. So, how can we best deal with these concerns?

A good first step is to acknowledge that such skepticism is totally understandable. In fact, it would be surprising if even a *single* proponent of more-participatory forms of democracy had never, in a moment of doubt, asked whether "the populace" should really be trusted with political power. Many elements in our culture invite negative views of "the average person on the street." Both our economic and biological models assume that humans are guided by the pursuit of a narrowly defined self-interest.[36] Given the prominence—in our societies, in our academic institutions and in our media—of economic thought and biological accounts of behavior, these end up playing an important role in disseminating and promoting this view of human beings. This dire image is compounded by the media's love affair with crime and other forms of abusive or gruesome behavior, which succeeds in terrifying and inspiring distrust in a significant number of us. It is a "dog-eat-dog" world out there, we are constantly reminded.

That is why we should always be careful not to judge those who have let themselves be swayed by this mosaic of gloomy views about humanity. Doing so will only further alienate them. Instead, we should focus on exploring two general, closely related questions. First, what, exactly, leads so many people to believe that elected politicians are better champions of the public interest than ordinary citizens? Second, what can help explain the prevalence of this dismal view of humankind, which makes us think so poorly of the strangers with whom we cross paths every day? By noticing and understanding the biases that lie at the root of these views, we stand a chance of realizing just how skewed these perceptions are.

---

[36] To be more precise, in the case of biology, behavior is understood as maximizing the dissemination of one's genes. Regardless of whether or not this constitutes a form of "self-interest," the resulting picture is equally dismal.

♦ ♦ ♦

Perhaps the most frequent argument justifying our reliance on an elected political class is that, compared to the average person on the street, professional politicians supposedly have superior decision-making skills. In short, they are smarter and more educated than most of us.

This might seem true at first glance, but we should take a moment to reflect on the factors that get in the way of us forming an accurate judgment of our elected leaders' "true" abilities. On what kinds of occasions (or in what settings) does the general public get to see them? Are we ever witness to their decision-making process? And what might color our perceptions of how competent, smart and knowledgeable they really are?

The defining characteristic of the modern politician is her (and her advisors') expertise in managing her public persona. This is not surprising. After all, why do politicians get elected in the first place? It is precisely by virtue of their ability to leave a positive impression on the general public. They are skilled public speakers, trained in the art of projecting an air of confidence and expertise during their public appearances. Many of the more-senior politicians also benefit from small armies of PR consultants and other "spin doctors" when meeting the media. So, when watching them on TV, we should remember that we are witnessing seasoned performers delivering a carefully staged performance that has a single goal: to convince us of their unquestionable competence for political duty.

In other words, the very system we use to select politicians is designed to hand the power to those who most successfully *give the impression* of being competent. For that reason, we should not be surprised when they deliver convincing performances. And, just as importantly, neither should we mistake those performances for evidence of actual competence.

Even when a politician displays true expertise about a topic, we still should be skeptical. Suppose that you are watching a politician being interviewed about an important current event. She evidently knows what she is talking about, and that prompts us to unconsciously make two unwarranted inferences.

First, we will tend to take that display of competence as indicative of her background expertise on that topic. We forget that, on most occasions, politicians are—just like the rest of us—quite ignorant about the substantive issues involved in any policy topic until they have (i) studied them and (ii) been extensively briefed by their assistants (and probably a few corporate lobbyists) about it. The fact that they discuss matters publicly only *after* that sort of preparation creates the illusion that they are astoundingly well-rounded, knowledgeable individuals.

Second, the positive impression caused by a politician's public display of expertise on a particular topic leads us to— often unconsciously—assume that she would have proved equally knowledgeable about other major policy topics if only the journalist had decided to quiz her on them instead. (This would be an instance of what psychologists call the "halo effect": making a positive judgment about someone predisposes us towards making *other* positive judgments about that person.)

The result is that we end up vastly overestimating how knowledgeable politicians are. And, perhaps even more perversely, we mistakenly learn to think of expertise in general policy matters as an almost "intrinsic" trait of politicians—that is, as something that they already possessed and brought to the job, rather than as something they *acquired* on the job. We take all of this as yet more evidence that they are somehow fundamentally better equipped for political duty than the rest of us.

It is also worth reflecting on just how "safe" most public appearances are for politicians. One of the central myths of our democracies is that a free press and competition among political parties ensure vigorous, adversarial oversight of those in power. The reality is that, in this day and age, politicians enjoy a remarkable level of control over their public appearances, including events such as press conferences at which they appear to be fielding questions "off the cuff." In fact, many such question and answer sessions are scripted, allowing politicians and their staff ample time to carefully rehearse them. Even when they are not scripted, the questions or challenges presented by opposition politicians or journalists are easy to predict, so adequate replies can be prepared beforehand, thus minimizing the chances of being caught off guard. If things become uncomfortable, non-answers—from the vanilla "I am not going to comment on that" to more sophisticated displays of logical/semantic play—are widely accepted and rarely challenged. With rare exceptions, neither opposition politicians nor journalists wish to be seen as "obnoxious" and, thus, choose to abide by the gentlemanly rules of the game. (After all, if they don't comply, their invitation to the next such event may be in jeopardy.) The result is mostly tame, ritualistic exchanges in which the public is served a mere *illusion* of democratic scrutiny, but which, in reality, present no threat to the public image of those in power.

And, although we like to think ourselves immune to such primitive forms of manipulation, our political institutions and the social norms surrounding the world of politics are rife with status cues that promote the view that our politicians are somehow *above* the rest of the citizenry. After all, these are people who work in the regal buildings that house our political institutions. They can be seen wearing expensive suits and riding in chauffeured cars. Some of them are so important that police or security guards are assigned to shield them from any unwanted interaction with members of the general public. Journalists—who many of us think of as "stand-ins" for us in the halls of power—are often seen addressing elected officials deferentially. Even their mere titles evoke an almost medieval sense of respect: *prime minister, president, secretary of state, chancellor*. All of this reinforces the common notion that the political class somehow levitates above our humble heads.

♦ ♦ ♦

Taken together, these different factors make it likely that the public perception of the political class will have a strong positive bias: we will tend to think of politicians *more positively* than they deserve.[37] An additional factor reinforcing this effect is a well-established finding in the field of cognitive psychology: people have an unconscious tendency to believe that the hierarchy in our society is ultimately justified. When people do well, most of us are inclined to look at them in a positive light and see them as *deserving* of what they got.[38] Psychologists have studied this bias for over 40 years and call it the "just-world phenomenon." Given the high status that the political class has traditionally enjoyed in our society, this idea suggests that the judgments we make of our leaders' abilities and competence levels will be

---

[37] Which, in itself, says a lot when you remember how poorly we tend to think of politicians in the first place. The positive bias discussed here implies that, in reality, they are even worse.

[38] Obviously, we can all name exceptions. Still, those exceptions bother us—and are, therefore, memorable—precisely because they violate our general expectation that, with a few bumps here and there, most people will get the outcomes that they justly deserve.

more positive than is warranted by the information generally available to the public—which, as argued above, is already heavily skewed in their favor.

◆ ◆ ◆

But if, even in light of all this, we still believe that relying exclusively on professional politicians allows for better public decision-making due to their supposed above-average intelligence and education, then perhaps we should be asking ourselves a different question.

Assume for a moment that professional politicians *were* indeed vastly smarter and more knowledgeable than the average citizen. Does that necessarily make them the right people to govern us?

History provides us with countless examples of highly skilled individuals in positions of power who, in spite of their intelligence and political experience, made terrible decisions. Strangely, we seem to have some difficulty absorbing this lesson. Most of us still place intelligence and expertise high on the list of essential traits when choosing whom to entrust with political power.

Perhaps the time has come for us to reconsider our notion of political competence, so that rather than basing our judgments strictly on notions such as intellectual finesse, leadership skills, etc., we also begin to recognize *reasonableness* and *public-spiritedness* as essential political virtues. If we reframe our picture of the true requirements for successful policy-making in this way, then any preconceived notion regarding the obvious superiority of professional politicians should begin to melt away.

◆ ◆ ◆

Now, let's examine the exceedingly negative view so many of us have of our fellow citizens. Where does it come from and what might explain it? Understanding this is helpful because it will make it easier to assuage concerns about the participation of ordinary citizens in politics.

Consider the origin of our mental image of "the person on the street." For the vast majority of us, our view of what is on the minds of people outside our immediate social circle is based largely on how the media portrays them. In particular, the expression "the average person" will often conjure unpleasant memories of ten-second clips of street interviews shown on prime-time TV news shows, often featuring irate—and, just as frequently, utterly inarticulate—"average" people.

Watching these, we should remember the purpose underlying the selection and editing of the particular clips that get aired. TV news—like much of the media in general—thrives on conflict, colorful displays of emotion and extreme views. Perhaps more crucially, consider the hothead who is assailed on the street by a TV crew and promised a brief appearance on that evening's newscast. Under these unusual and tense circumstances, he is much more likely to spew some unconsidered opinions than if he were participating in a citizen panel deliberating on the same issue over the course of multiple days. It is the same distinction that VS Naipaul made in an interview when asked to reflect on the nature of a writer's work:

> *There are two ways of talking. One is the easy way, where you talk lightly, and the other one is the considered way.* The considered way is what I have put my name to. I wouldn't put my name to the easy thoughts, because *you can often have out-rageous views, passionate views,* and *that's the source of your thoughts, eventually. But when*

*they occur, they are very rough and brutal. And
so a lot of writers' time is spent in working out or
refining coarse thought.*

We can also formulate this using the terminology popularized in Daniel Kahneman's recent book, *Thinking, Fast and
Slow*. According to this framework, we essentially have two
different decision-making systems. The first ("system 1") is
fast and intuitive, while the second ("system 2") is slower
and more logical. Nearly all of our exposure to the political
thoughts and preferences of other ordinary citizens is based
exclusively on the output of their "system 1." Citizen
deliberation, on the other hand, is all about capturing the
output of their "system 2" through collaborative analysis
and reflection.

Perhaps more intuitively, we all know from our own experience that context plays a huge role in shaping our behavior.
Different settings provide us with different behavioral cues
and we might, as a result, act in almost unrecognizable ways.
I am *not* the same person at the pub Friday night than I am at
a work meeting early Monday morning. Similarly, everything
about interacting with the media prompts attitudes and
behaviors that are at the opposite extreme of those elicited by
a well-structured citizen deliberation process. This means that
whatever we learn by watching ordinary citizens in the first
setting (appearing on the media and making unconsidered
remarks) is a poor indication of how the same people would
behave in the second (engaging in actual political decision-
making in a deliberative setting).

The same thought applies to any concern one might feel
regarding the casual, off-the-cuff comments made by friends
or acquaintances as they scan the headlines of a tabloid or
after having watched the news on TV. Like other potent
psychoactive substances, most of the media is meant to

arouse strong immediate emotions in its consumers. Therefore, we should not be surprised when people react to news coverage by adopting rather extreme attitudes, and we should not mistake these attitudes for the contributions those same individuals could make in a deliberative setting. Both in the case of those *appearing* in the media and of those *consuming* it, less-than-thoughtful attitudes are better understood as a *consequence* of our current political regime—in which citizens' political expression is generally reduced to such powerless rants, on- or off-screen—than as indication of the true political potential of ordinary citizens.[39]

◆ ◆ ◆

Another common concern is whether ordinary citizens can be *trusted* with power. Obviously, we will always need constitutional checks on political institutions. But any specific concerns on this front can usually be dealt with by confronting doubters with a simple question: who do you think is more honest—the average career politician or the average citizen?

◆ ◆ ◆

The fact that panels of randomly chosen citizens already play a crucial role in a vast number of countries should also ease our concerns. Trial by jury is commonly used for the most serious criminal offenses, most notably in countries such as the US and the UK. People in these countries do not generally find it problematic that, should they be charged with a serious crime, a randomly chosen sample of their

---

[39] Carne Ross explores this idea in greater depth in his book *The Leaderless Revolution: How Ordinary People Will Take Power and Change Politics in the 21st Century*.

fellow citizens will determine their guilt or innocence. So, if groups of ordinary citizens are deemed competent and trustworthy enough for decisions that can affect human lives in such a drastic way, why should we not trust them with similarly important functions in the legislative and executive branches?

◆ ◆ ◆

Let's step back for a moment and try to understand what these two main obstacles to democratic reform have in common. One way to think about them is to observe that they are both expressions of the same sentiment: fear in face of uncertainty. In the first case, we are dealing with the fear of not knowing how the world would react if we embraced a more democratic form of doing politics. In the second, it is the fear of not knowing what would happen if we had ordinary citizens involved in policy-making.

These are understandable concerns. Fear of the unknown is something that plagues all of us. One way to assuage these concerns is to think about how much—and what kind of— certainty our current regime ensures us. There is plenty of certainty, but it is *the wrong kind*: it is the near-certainty of continuing down our current path. It is the certainty that politicians will continue to make decisions that fly in the face of the public interest and place all of us at risk through a combination of economic instability (under a false promise of continued growth), environmental irresponsibility, and the looming populist threat (already manifested in the most recent Greek, Italian and British elections) attributable to the growing alienation of large parts of the citizenry.

Faced with this choice, it is blindly following our current course that seems foolhardy. Remember that all advocates of the establishment who belittle the prospect of meaningful democratic reform must answer for the economic, environmental and political situation we find ourselves in. In other words, the onus is on the apologists of mainstream politics.

♦ ♦ ♦

I want to emphasize that none of the central ideas in this book is novel. Citizen deliberation, electoral reform and abrogative referendums have all been put into practice in several parts of the world. So we know that, as individual building blocks for democratic reform, they constitute sane and safe choices.

In fact, a few might even *fault* these proposals precisely for *not* having a track record of, just by themselves, immediately bringing about radical change. But, in most people's eyes, practical and safe reforms are to be lauded since caution is obviously warranted, and their demonstrated "safety" is sure to help when campaigning for their adoption. This does not mean, however, that these reforms would fail to bring about a radically more democratic future.

Why? Because, so far, they have been tried only in isolation and always in the context of traditional representative democracies, where an established political class remained safely at the helm. It is only through the *combination* of several of these measures — through a concerted attempt at meaningful reform — that we truly stand a chance of gaining control over politicians and the interests they represent.

Perhaps even more importantly, citizens will also need time to adapt and learn how to use these new democratic tools. Improving our democratic institutions certainly is a step in the right direction, but it is only through what Nobel laureate Amartya Sen called the "effective practice" of democracy that real change will occur. Therefore, we shouldn't expect to feel the full effect of these reforms overnight.

♦ ♦ ♦

Still on the topic of change, it is also worth reflecting on how different our political and business cultures are. We live in what is essentially a global political monoculture. Deviations from the mainstream way of doing things are nearly impossible by virtue of our governance mechanisms. We are taught that this sameness equates "political stability" and that it is even something positive.

When it comes to the business world, though, fostering entrepreneurship and innovation is commonly hailed as the cornerstone of economic growth. It is from that diversity of approaches that great solutions eventually emerge. This plurality is the path to prosperity, we are told.

Given the failure of our political institutions on a level that is, by now, nearly universally recognized, the argument for reasoned and well-informed democratic experimentalism is an easy one. The monoculture we have been relying on is dying. The time has come for us to try something else.

♦ ♦ ♦

No matter how we do it, though, it will take time and effort to define exactly how our improved political institutions should look. In particular, we will have to design deliberative institutions in a way that will reliably bring out the best thinking in citizens. Fortunately, we know from experience that this can be done, as the examples of British Columbia and Oregon attest. It is only by ignoring these success stories that this task might seem impossible.

Provided that we succeed in fighting pessimism, change—the kind that *really* matters, *not* the kind invariably promised by politicians on the campaign trail—is within our grasp. I hope that this book has inspired you to want to know more and to participate in this process. One way to begin is to join us on **http://rebootdemocracy.org**. It is a simple website with a simple purpose: to serve as a meeting point for all those who want to take part in building a more democratic future. See you there.

POSTSCRIPT

An experience late last year—after I had completed this book—reinforced for me the idea that a shared perception that we need to "try something else" is not enough. As the following account will convey, we also need to intelligently manage our different understandings of what that "something else" might stand for.

On a mid-November evening, I attended what promised to be an interesting roundtable in Palácio Pombal, an old palace in my native Lisbon that now houses a young, vibrant cultural association. The event was named "What good are large demonstrations?" It brought together representatives of the four social movements responsible for organizing the largest street protests in Portugal since the years immediately following the 1974 democratic revolution. Contributing to my high expectations was the fact that one of the most insightful columnists in the Portuguese media had been invited to moderate the discussion.

I don't know what others took away from the event, but what struck me the most was how easy it is to lose sight of a common objective. In this room, there were, perhaps, 40 or 50 people, all of whom had a remarkable amount in common. They opposed the austerity program being imposed on the country. They agreed on the need for sustained protests to increase the pressure on the government. They opposed "sectarianism" and believed in the need for cooperation when organizing future protests. By any rational account, this should have been enough for them to build a shared agenda well into the foreseeable future. However, that was not what happened. Instead, they spent most of that evening attacking each other.

♦ ♦ ♦

What might explain that? Identity, the powerful psychological mechanism that came up several times in this book, certainly played a large role. Most of the participants were members of a variety of tightly-knit groups, each of them possessing a set of strong beliefs that made for equally strong identities. In a setting that made those identities salient, tensions easily flared up.

But let's try to see what might lie behind these antagonistic political identities. Why are these movements—most of which did not even exist five years ago—recreating the pathological dynamics typical of leftist parties throughout the twentieth century? The in-fighting, the propensity to splinter, the deep animosity that is almost impossible for an outsider to grasp—where do they come from?

I realized that these are the pathologies that inevitably afflict movements aiming at broader political change. If we sit down together to figure out what the world should look like (and there are no external constraints preventing disagreement from causing a group to splinter), we will end up with as many utopias as there are participants. And not just that: even if two of us happen to share the same utopia, we are still bound to disagree on the best path to take us there. Since we face not only a multitude of final destinations, but also so many different paths to get us to each of them, it's easy to see how clashes will erupt. That is what I witnessed that evening, and it did not bode well for any attempt at meaningful reform.

◆ ◆ ◆

So, have I succumbed to pessimism in the end? Not at all. My point in telling you this short tale is that we need to be aware of these pitfalls—and clever in the way we navigate around them. In particular, it is worth asking ourselves if there are there any practical lessons we can derive from this all-too-common story.

One possibility, I believe, would be for us to advocate *a process* for reforming our democracies rather than just a handful of specific solutions. Perhaps we could focus on launching a project that would enable *society as a whole* to intelligently decide how to reshape the political system—as opposed to hammering out the details ourselves and then trying to sell those ideas to the public. If done right, this approach could make it substantially easier for those who care deeply about these matters to act together. Collaboration would be possible as long as we agreed on the intrinsic soundness of that decision process.

Contrast this with the endless internal discussions that would ensue if a movement to reform our democracies had to decide on a concrete, detailed program to promote. How could we expect the members of this group to deal with the myriad options available to them when delineating the precise workings of their dream democracy? We'd soon be left with, at most, one or two people in the room—all the others having gone off to find (or launch) a political group that shared their *exact* vision of the future. Agreeing on utopias is tricky that way.

Such a strategy would have other advantages, too. We are all wary of others trying to sell us their own pet solutions. As Alain de Botton observed, in most domains, we'd much rather have ideas appear to be the result of common sense or collective wisdom than a gift bestowed upon us by an enlightened few. This means that those aiming to reform our democracies can probably do better than to go around preaching the virtues of the particular solution(s) they favor. Thus, it might be preferable to let the actual solutions emerge from a public process of some sort.

It will come as no surprise that I believe citizen deliberation to be perfectly suited for conducting such a process. In particular, holding a large citizens' assembly on how to reform our political institutions would allow us to identify which concrete solutions to enact in a way that both side-steps political elites and mitigates the risks of decisions made with inadequate thought or reflection. The assembly's proposed solutions could then be presented to the electorate for approval in a referendum. The bulk of those who have an earnest desire to democratize our way of doing politics should be able to support such a plan, confident that the intrinsic merits of the proposals they personally favor would win them the support of the citizens' assembly.

The case for this strategy is bolstered by the fact that several citizens' assemblies have been convened precisely to decide on issues of political reform. In addition to the case of British Columbia, over the last decade, similar processes took place—with varying degrees of independence from the local political class—in Ontario, the Netherlands and Ireland. In all of these, the focus was strictly on electoral reform, but there is, of course, no reason to restrict the assembly's mandate in that way.

Made in the USA
San Bernardino, CA
24 August 2014